HX
546
.S625
2005

Smith,
Women and socialism

DISCARD

MAR 04 2013

Women and Socialism

Women and Socialism
Essays on Women's Liberation

Sharon Smith

Chicago, Illinois

©2005 Sharon Smith

Published in 2005 by Haymarket Books
P.O. Box 180165, Chicago IL 60618
www.haymarketbooks.org

ISBN-10: 1-931859-11-6
ISBN-13: 9-781-931859-110

Cover design by Amy Balkin
Cover photo: March for Womens' Lives,
Washington, D.C., April 25, 2004 (Nikki Kahn/KRT)

Library of Congress Cataloging-in-Publication Data
Smith, Sharon
Women and socialism : essays on women's liberation / Sharon Smith.
p. cm.
Includes bibliographical references (p.) and index.
ISBN-10: 1-931859-11-6 (pbk. 10 digit)
ISBN-13: 978-1-931859-11-0 (pbk. 13 digit)
1. Women and socialism. 2. Women's rights. 3. Feminism. 4.
Women—Religious aspects—Islam. I. Title.
HX546.S625 2005
305.42—dc22
                                    2005004324

Printed in Canada
10 9 8 7 6 5 4 3 2

Contents

Is This Post-feminism— or Anti-feminism?

CONVENTIONAL WISDOM holds that women's oppression is the product of a bygone era, and ideas of women's liberation are outdated relics of that era. The women's movement accomplished its goals a long time ago, according to mainstream pundits, and U.S. society has entered the enlightened phase of "post-feminism." In this context, demanding any further advancement for women's rights would be a colossal act of selfishness.

But the evidence offered by the mass media for gender parity typically measures the number of women carrying briefcases to work, rather than how average women are faring.

To be sure, between 1972 and 1992, the proportion of managerial jobs held by women more than doubled, from 20 percent to 46 percent.[1] And a small number of women have now advanced to the upper echelons of corporations and government institutions. Condoleezza Rice is the U.S. secretary of state, and New York Senator Hillary Clinton is under consideration as the Democratic Party's presidential nominee in 2008. Although a small number of individual women have achieved real power, their accomplishments do not represent genuine advancement for the vast majority of women—either in the United States or globally.

The advancement of the few within the system, in fact, is fraught with contradiction for the many who do not benefit from the system as a whole. Condoleezza Rice is now one of the most powerful women in the world, key to shaping foreign policy for the world's only superpower. But the millions of women—in Iraq and elsewhere—who have been the victims of U.S. war and occupation have no reason to celebrate Rice's career success. In another irony, the CEO of Playboy Enterprises today is a woman, not a man. Christie Hefner, daughter of Hugh, has been in charge of this highly profitable corporation since 1988. Although a woman is now earning a seven-figure salary to run the corporation, *Playboy* remains a potent symbol of the sexual objectification of women's bodies—a key component of women's oppression.

In a number of respects, women's oppression has grown worse since the women's movement of the 1970s that supposedly liberated women. Although the United States remains the richest country in the world, the gap between rich and poor is higher now than at any time since the Great Depression. And working-class women have won precious few reforms from the government that so values freedom of en-

terprise. Paid maternity leave for any length of time is un-
heard of in the United States—even though women workers
in most other countries (including Iraq under Saddam Hus-
sein) have received government-mandated maternity leave
for decades. Payment for child care is the third largest expenditure, after housing and food, for working families with
children in the United States, without the substantial government subsidies that exist elsewhere in the world.[2]

Women's wages in the United States now average roughly
75 percent of men's. This is much higher than the 59 percent
figure in 1979. But this relative increase is due less to rising
women's wages than to the dramatic fall in men's real wages
over the last several decades. In addition, more women are
working longer hours at year-round, full-time jobs.[3] This "advance" is hardly a reason to celebrate for either gender.

Black women and Latinas have not shared even in this
small rise in wages. In 1998, for example, the average working Latina earned only 50 percent of what the average white
man earns. Moreover, the effects of racism neutralize gender advantages for Black men and Latinos. An African-Amer-
ican man with a master's degree, for example, earned just
$321 more than a white woman with a master's in 1998—but
$17,854 less than a white man with a master's.[4]

And the overall wage disparity between women and men
increases dramatically when women's wages are compared
with men's over the long term. A study of men's and

women's wages between 1983 and 1998 showed women earning an average of $274,000 to men's $723,000.[5] As Jennifer Roesch noted in the *International Socialist Review*, "In other words, taken over fifteen prime working years, women averaged $0.38 for a man's dollar. This study more accurately measures the impact of women's oppression because it takes into account the cumulative effect on women's earnings from having to balance work and family."[6]

Women's oppression has grown in other respects as well. Although abortion has been legal in the United States since 1973, it was more accessible to women twenty years ago than it is today. A wide range of legal restrictions have been passed at both state and federal levels—including bans on Medicaid funding for poor women's abortions, mandatory waiting periods, parental notification requirements, and most recently, the deceptively titled "partial birth abortion" ban. Today, at least 85 percent of counties nationwide have no abortion provider.[7]

These restrictions have not only made abortion much more difficult to obtain but have eroded the very notion that women should have the right to control their own bodies and reproductive lives—the central demand of the abortion rights movement in the 1970s. With George W. Bush's 2004 victory, an emboldened Christian Right has launched an assault on gay marriage, and a renewed offensive on the right to choose. Right-wing crackpot Jerry Falwell launched the

Faith and Values Coalition a week after the election, as a "21st century version of the Moral Majority."[8] Christian congregations ran the get-out-the-vote machine for the Republican Party in 2004, and they immediately demanded payback for Bush's victory, in the form of concrete progress toward outlawing abortion. More than three decades after the Supreme Court's 1973 *Roe v. Wade* decision that made abortion legal, the right to choose is once again in peril.

The twenty-five-year backlash

"Post-feminism" is a term brimming with hypocrisy—promoted primarily by those who oppose the struggle for women's rights. For more than twenty years, conservative pundits within the mass media have played a central role in providing the ideological fodder for reversing the gains of the women's movement, popularizing a range of anti-feminist ideas. Journalist Susan Faludi brilliantly documented the first decade of this process in her 1991 book, *Backlash: The Undeclared War Against American Women.*[9] This backlash has only accelerated over the last decade, as part of a conservative effort to discredit feminism.

The mass media has played a key role in hyping the anti-feminist themes of self-proclaimed "experts" who lack convincing evidence and conduct "research" with suspicious methodology. Through sheer repetition, however, these themes have been absorbed into popular culture.

Career women were early targets in the war on feminism, when the mass media advanced the theory that women professionals who postponed marriage or children until they reached their thirties or beyond looked back and realized they had made a terrible mistake. Using faulty evidence from a Harvard-Yale study on marriage, the media declared a "man shortage" crisis in the 1980s. *Newsweek* magazine went so far as to claim in 1986 that a single woman in her forties was more likely to be "killed by a terrorist" than ever marry. Although it was subsequently proven that the study was in error—it turned out there were actually substantially more unmarried men than women in this age group—the damage had been done.[10]

Working mothers, on the other hand, have been fed a steady diet of guilt for leaving their children in day care over the last three decades. Although the majority of women with young children work outside the home today, this line of attack has not abated. The latest installment is *Home-Alone America: The Hidden Toll of Day Care, Behavioral Drugs and Other Parent Substitutes*, by Mary Eberstadt, research fellow for Stanford's Hoover Institution. The book's front cover depicts a woman dressed in a business suit leaving for work as her small child desperately clings to her. Eberstadt blames working mothers, single mothers, and divorced parents for such wide-ranging social problems as child obesity, teen pregnancy, and sexually transmitted diseases. "Over the past few decades, more and more children have spent considerably less time in the company of their parents or other relatives, and numerous fundamental measures of their well-being have simultaneously gone into what once would have been judged scandalous decline," Eberstadt argues.[11]

More recently, the backlash has incorporated a new claim—that women professionals have been quitting their jobs in droves to embrace stay-at-home motherhood. In October 2003, the *New York Times Magazine* featured a cover story, "The Opt-Out Revolution," describing a small group of white middle-class Yale and Princeton graduates who decided to quit their careers because they are more fulfilled by full-time motherhood. One of the women interviewed argues, "I think some of us are swinging to a place where we enjoy, and can admit we enjoy, the stereotypical role of female/mother/caregiver. I think we were born with those feelings." Although the article describes the experience of a mere handful of privileged women, its conclusion is sweeping: "Why don't women run the world? Maybe it's because they don't want to."[12]

As in the 1950s, today's emphasis on the importance of motherhood has—albeit ironically—coincided with greater sexual objectification of women's bodies in popular culture, placing enormous pressure on women of all ages to conform to beauty standards and sexual ideals manufactured on Wall Street and in Hollywood. The beauty ideal today, however, has changed drastically from the voluptuous Marilyn Monroe (size 12), to the super-thin supermodel (size 2–4).

Increasingly, the beauty ideal is actually manufactured, through liposuction, cosmetic surgery, and Botox injections. The Web site for the ABC television show *Extreme Makeover* promises that the plastic surgery makeover offered to participants is "a real-life fairy tale in which their wishes come true, not just to change their looks, but their lives and destinies." As Australian journalist Emma Young observed, leaders of the $35 billion cosmetics industry now "promote moisturizers notable for their anti-aging pretensions with advertising that compares their wares with the surgeon's knife."[13]

Meanwhile, the occurrence of eating disorders such as anorexia and bulimia has skyrocketed among younger women. Since Twiggy came on the fashion scene in the late 1960s (weighing in at 91 pounds on a 5' 7" frame), the undernourished female has been the popular ideal. In the 1980s, fashion model icons weighed 23 percent less than the average female.[14] In the 1980s, however, the typical size for fashion models was a 6 or an 8. Today's models are required to fit into a size 2 or 4. As modeling executive Jennifer Venditti explained in a 2001 *Cosmopolitan* article, "That's the designers' dream size. On their sketches, the body is like a hanger. The smaller the sample, the better it drapes.... It's almost like the body is not present."[15]

In the United States, a woman between the ages of eighteen and thirty-four has a 7 percent chance of being as slim as a catwalk model and a 1 percent chance of being as thin as a supermodel.[16] Yet the image permeates popular culture with unrealistic images that negatively affect self-esteem among females from a very young age. By the age of ten, 80 percent of girls in the United States have already tried to diet to lose weight.[17] And at any given time, 50 percent of American women are in the midst of dieting.[18]

"Body-type trends go up and down as often as hemlines," noted Michael Gross, author of *Model: The Ugly Business of Beautiful Women.* "We've seen body ideals go from buxom to flat-chested, from tall to petite, and every now and then, you'll see the season of the ass."[19] The reduction of women's sexuality in popular culture to a sum total of body parts, instead of belonging to a whole person, helps to explain the prevailing acceptance in society today, among both men and women, that women's bodies exist for the pleasure of men. This notion is reinforced not only through the flourishing pornography industry, which took in $10 billion in the United States last year,[20] but more pervasively through commercial advertising, which uses women's bodies and acts of seduction to sell everything from beer and automobiles to movie tickets.

The objectification of women's bodies both demeans women and dehumanizes sexuality—reflected in the high incidence of rape and battery suffered by women the world over. Roughly one in every three women worldwide has been beaten, raped, or otherwise abused in her lifetime—and up to

70 percent have never told anyone else about the abuse they have suffered. This conclusion was based on a review of over one thousand articles in scientific journals and national reports conducted by Johns Hopkins University researchers, published in the journal *Population Reports* in 1999.[21]

The issue of rape—and date rape in particular—has been central to the right-wing backlash over the last decade. Conservative pundits have repeatedly accused feminists of creating a "victim" consciousness among women, causing college-aged women to falsely accuse men of date rape. Harvard graduate Katie Roiphe made a big splash with her 1993 book, *The Morning After: Sex, Fear and Feminism*, blaming feminists for creating an atmosphere of "rape crisis melodrama" that greatly exaggerated the problem of date rape on college campuses.[22] *Newsweek* magazine ran a ten-page spread on the evils of "sexual correctness" in 1994, with the headline, "Stop Whining," and a feature story by Republican consultant Mary Matalin admonishing women for filing "frivolous" date rape and sexual harassment claims that "clog the system."[23] Right-wing syndicated columnist Kathleen Parker regularly ridicules the problem of date rape, with comments such as, "The biggest myth that won't die is that one of four college women is raped on campuses each year.... If 25 percent of Daddy's little girls were being sexually assaulted at college, there wouldn't be any girls on campus."[24]

The figures Parker holds in such contempt are based on

a broad study conducted in the 1980s by *Ms.* magazine under the direction of psychologist Mary P. Koss. The study surveyed six thousand students at thirty-two colleges in the United States, and found that one in four college women surveyed had been a victim of rape or attempted rape—a figure now widely accepted, even by the U.S. Department of Justice.[25] In a separate survey, 43 percent of college-aged men admitted to having used coercive behavior to obtain sex, including ignoring a woman's protest, using physical aggression, and forcing intercourse, but did not consider it to be "rape."[26] Furthermore, only an estimated 31 percent of rapes and sexual assaults were reported to law enforcement officials in 1996—fewer than one in every three.[27] Date rape is not a figment of the imaginations of "hysterical" feminists, but an indisputable reality for women in the United States.

Which way forward?

The backlash has taken a severe toll on women's rights, and feminism must be defended against any and all attacks from the right wing. The women's liberation movement of the 1970s involved many thousands of women—and men—in fighting for equality for women, and it raised the aspirations for millions of working-class women. The movement won crucial reforms—most notably, abortion rights—and raised demands for equal pay and government-subsidized child care.

At the same time, those striving today to resurrect the

fight for women's liberation must examine the reasons why the women's movement a generation ago did not *win* real equality for women. Even the Equal Rights Amendment (ERA)—which would have guaranteed only the most basic legal equality for women—has wallowed in Congress for three decades without passage.

This book is an attempt to address the theoretical weaknesses of feminism while offering a Marxist framework for understanding women's oppression. The chapters are updated essays written over the course of the last decade that examine current issues from a historical perspective—while looking forward to the future struggle for women's liberation.

The first chapter, "The Origin of Women's Oppression," explores the root of women's oppression—and all forms of inequality and oppression—in the rise of class society. It is an attempt to refute the argument made by some feminists that women's oppression has existed as long as human society, and to further explore the many ways in which economic factors have played a role in shaping the personal aspects of the unequal relationship between women and men.

"Abortion Rights: The Socialist Case," the second chapter, explains the urgent need for women to control their own bodies as a precondition for equality with men. Although this fundamental right was won by the women's liberation movement in 1973, it has been under attack ever since. This chapter examines why the Christian Right has been so successful

in eroding the right to choose, while the pro-choice movement has been severely set back.

Chapter three, "What Ever Happened to Feminism?" con-
fronts the middle-class loyalties of mainstream feminism.
These have become more evident in recent years, but can be
traced to the founders of "second wave" feminism in the
1960s. Mainstream feminism has never been able to ade-
quately address the issues of greatest concern to working-
class women—and in many respects, has never actually
tried—because it aims to advance women's rights within the
system, rather than fundamentally transform it.

The fourth chapter, "Women and Islam," was written as a
rebuttal to the widespread belief in the West that Islam is
uniquely and barbarically oppressive to women. George W.
Bush hypocritically claimed to be "liberating" Afghan women
while the United States was bombing Afghanistan in 2001,
but little has changed for women in "liberated" Afghanistan
today. And although Western values have been held up as a
model for Islamic women to emulate, Western women are
also oppressed in ways that may differ in form, but not in
substance. In fact, women's oppression within Islam shares
its historical roots with both Christianity and Judaism.

The final chapter, "Women and Socialism," lays out the
theoretical foundation for fighting women's oppression first
argued by Marx, and later more fully developed by Engels.
Russian revolutionaries in the early twentieth century

demonstrated the commitment by Marxists to winning women's liberation in practice. Although the Russian Revolution was short-lived, it remains to this day the greatest step toward winning genuine equality for women since class society arose. It gave the world a glimpse of the potential for the working class to fight to end war, exploitation, and oppression for all of humanity.

This book is offered in the spirit of collaboration with all those involved in the ongoing fight for women's liberation.

Sharon Smith
March 2004

CHAPTER 1

The Origin of Women's Oppression

HOW CAN we end women's oppression? This question can only be answered by posing yet another question: why are women oppressed? Unless we determine the source of women's oppression, we don't know who or what needs changing. This, the "woman question," has been a source of controversy for well over a century. Karl Marx and Frederick Engels located the origin of women's oppression in the rise of class society. Their analysis of women's oppression was not something that was tagged on as an afterthought to their analysis of class society but was integral to it from the very beginning. When Marx wrote *The Communist Manifesto* in 1848, ideas of women's liberation were already a central part of revolutionary socialist theory:

> The bourgeois sees in his wife a mere instrument of production. He hears that [under communism] the instruments of

production are to be exploited in common, and, naturally, can come to no other conclusion than that the lot of being common to all will likewise fall to women.

He has not even a suspicion that the real point aimed at [by communists] is to do away with the status of women as mere instruments of production.[1]

Marx and Engels developed a theory of women's oppression over a lifetime, culminating in the publication of *The Origin of the Family, Private Property and the State* in 1884.[2] Engels wrote *The Origin* after Marx's death, but it was a joint collaboration, as he used Marx's detailed notes along with his own.

The theory put forward in *The Origin* is based largely upon the pioneering research of the nineteenth-century anthropologist Lewis Henry Morgan. Morgan's research, published in 1877 in a 560-page volume called *Ancient Society*, was the first materialist attempt to understand the evolution of human social organization. He discovered, through extensive contact with the Iroquois Indians in upstate New York, a kinship system that took a completely different form than the modern nuclear family. Within it, the Iroquois lived in relative equality and women exercised a great deal of authority. This discovery inspired Morgan to study other societies, and, in so doing, he learned that other Native American societies located thousands of miles from the Iroquois used remarkably similar kinship structures. This led him to argue that human society had evolved through successive stages, based upon the development of the "successive arts of subsistence."[3] While some of Morgan's anthropological data is now outdated, a wealth of more recent anthropology has provided ample evidence to support his basic evolutionary framework.[4]

Engels built upon Morgan's theory in *The Origin* to develop, as the title implies, a theory of how the rise of class society led to both the rise of the state, which represents the interests of the ruling class in the day-to-day class struggle, and the rise of the family, as the means by which the first ruling classes possessed and passed on private wealth. In order to appreciate fully the pathbreaking contribution of Engels' (not to mention Morgan's) work, it is only necessary to realize that Darwin laid out his theory of human evolution just a few years earlier, first with the publication of *Origin of Species* in 1859, followed by *Descent of Man* in 1871. The first early human skeletal remains were not even discovered until 1856![5] For this reason, some of Engels' specific formulations have needed revision in light of data that were unavailable in his time.

This in no way diminishes the lasting importance of Engels' contribution. He developed a historical analysis that locates the source of women's oppression. In so doing, he provided a strategy for ending that oppression. It is no exaggeration to say that Engels' work has defined the terms of debate around the origin of women's oppression for the last hundred years. Most writers on the subject of women's oppression have set out either to support or reject Marxist theory as laid out by Engels in *The Origin of the Family, Private Property and the State* since it was published. Here, I hope to summarize the essence of his theory and touch upon the points of controversy.

Sexist Neanderthals?

While the battle lines have been drawn around widely divergent points of view, socialists most often find themselves alone in challenging the assumption that women's oppression is due, to a greater or lesser extent, to men's long-standing need to dominate and oppress women. This assumption is held both by traditional male chauvinists seeking to prove a vaguely defined tendency in men to dominate women (and also a vaguely defined tendency in women to nurture and therefore submit to domination), as well as many feminists seeking to prove much the same thing. The argument is rarely a purely biological one over testosterone levels. Yet, whether stated or implied, assumptions about biology and human nature lurk just beneath the surface of this debate.[6]

The specific explanations for women's oppression range far and wide—some are downright preposterous and most are based far more on mere speculation than on any concrete evidence. The most common theories have been based on the assumption that men's greater physical strength leads them to be more aggressive (the logic being, presumably, that men dominate women simply because they can). The familiar childhood image of furry Neanderthals dragging their women by the hair from cave to cave certainly seems to be based on this false biological assumption.

Much of the debate about the origin of women's oppression has taken place within the field of anthropology, the study of human societies. Far from an objective science, anthropological study carries with it all the subjective baggage of its researchers' own cultural prejudices. The most obvious is the male chauvinism that dominated the field until a few decades ago, which led most anthropologists to assume that all the important functions in any given society were performed by men. Eleanor Burke Leacock cited one clear-cut example in her book, *Myths of Male Dominance*, from a passage by the anthropologist Robin Fox that was written as if it was only for a male audience:

> For in behavior as in anatomy, the strength of our lineage lay in a relatively generalized structure. It was precisely because we did not specialize like our baboon cousins that we had to contrive solutions involving the control and exchange of females.[7]

Until the women's movement of the late 1960s began to challenge male chauvinism, sexist assumptions provided the basis for broad generalizations. Claude Levi-Strauss, a leading anthropologist within the structuralist school, goes so far as to argue that "human society...is primarily a masculine society." He argues that the "exchange of women" is a "practi-

cally universal" feature of human society, in which men obtain women from other men—from fathers, brothers, and
other male relatives. Moreover, he asserts that "the deep
polygamous tendency, which exists among all men, always
makes the number of available women seem insufficient."
Therefore, "the most desirable women must form a minority." Because of this, "the demand for women is an actual
fact, or to all intents and purposes, always in a state of dise-
quilibrium and tension."[8] According to Levi-Strauss, then,
women have been the passive victims of men's sexual aggression since the beginning of human society.

Likewise, Western observers have frequently brought
along their own cultural biases (including, often, cultural
chauvinism) when they study hunter-gatherer or horticultural
societies. Customs are measured using a Western yardstick,
rather than trying to understand the unique value system of a
particular culture. For example, the common practice among
Eskimo women of sleeping with male visitors is often inter-
preted as an example of Eskimo women's low status—of
women offered up as gifts or property. Yet, this might or
might not be true. As Leacock points out, this is an "ethnocen-
tric reading which presumes that a woman does not (since
she should not) enjoy sex play with any but her 'real' husband
and which refuses to recognize that variety in sexual relations
is entertaining to women (where not circumscribed by all
manner of taboos) as well as to men."[9] In and of itself, this sex-

ual custom tells little about women's status in Eskimo society today—when it is fairly integrated into the capitalist system—much less, what women's status has been historically.

Theories abound that superimpose the features of a pre-class world onto societies that have lived for decades or even centuries under colonial domination. Marvin Harris, who has written a series of popular books on the origins of human societies, is a typical example of a writer who engages in this sort of speculation. Harris's theory rests on his assertion that "male supremacy" is a direct result of warfare and female infanticide, which he says early societies used to prevent population growth from depleting the surrounding environment. He admits, however, "Unfortunately, the data needed to test my predictions about the rise and fall of the intensity of warfare in relation to growth and the splitting up of specific villages have not yet been collected."

Yet, lack of empirical evidence in no way dampens his enthusiasm for his hypothesis. Moreover, Harris drew many of his conclusions based upon his studies of a group of war-prone Yanomamo who live on the border between Brazil and Venezuela, in which the men brutally dominate the women. As other writers have pointed out, however, other groups of Yanomamo are quite peaceful. Moreover, in all likelihood, this group of Yanomamo did not develop its propensity for warfare until 1758, when they fought off the first group of

Spanish and Portuguese explorers searching for slaves—in other words, until the onset of colonialism.[10]

Feminist stick-bending

Many feminist writers have been equally guilty of shaping the evidence to fit the theory. For example, Sherry Ortner argues in "Is Female to Male as Nature Is to Culture?" that, historically, women's capacity to give birth brought them closer to "nature," while men's capacity for warfare allowed them to dominate in the realm of "culture." On this basis, she makes the sweeping generalization that "everywhere, in every known culture, women are considered in some degree inferior to men." But she is short on evidence—and that which she offers is far from definitive. For example, she cites a 1930s study of a matrilineal American Indian society, the Crow. Although Ortner admits that in most respects Crow women hold positions of relatively high authority, she cites the Crow's taboo toward women during menstruation as evidence that they are nevertheless regarded as inferiors. Among other things, menstruating women are not allowed to touch either a wounded man or a man starting on a war party.[11]

This fairly commonplace practice of isolating menstruating women in primitive societies is often touted by feminists as evidence that women's reproductive powers are a source of fear and contempt universally. But they are not. For one thing, some hunter-gatherer societies have no menstrual

taboos at all. In others, men try to imitate women's reproductive powers. And, as Stephanie Coontz and Peta Henderson have pointed out, this interpretation of menstrual taboos
leaves "the impression that women are [viewed as] unclean
or evil instead of recognizing that certain substances, such
as blood, are considered dangerous, whether shed by
women or men" in many societies.[12]

To be sure, some feminist anthropologists—particularly
socialist-feminists, like Coontz and Henderson quoted
above—have contributed to our understanding of women's
oppression historically, and in some cases have helped to further develop Engels' theory.[13] And some feminist anthropologists have contributed extensive data helping to substantiate
Engels' claim of the existence of pre-class egalitarian societies, such as Patricia Draper's study of !Kung society in
Southern Africa and Judith Brown's research on the Iroquois.

But, in its purest form, much of feminist theory rests
upon no more than supposition—the range of which is limited only by the imaginations of its authors. Depending upon
who is doing the writing, men dominate women because
they hold women in contempt for their ability to bear children—or because they are jealous of women's ability to bear
children. Men oppress women because long ago women
formed a powerful matriarchy, which was overthrown—or
because men have always been a tyrannical patriarchy.
Gerda Lerner argues in her book, *The Creation of Patriarchy*,

"Feminists, beginning with Simone de Beauvoir…[have explained women's oppression] as caused by either male biology or male psychology." She goes on to describe a sampling of feminist theories, all of which border on the outlandish:

> Thus, Susan Brownmiller sees man's ability to rape women leading to their propensity to rape women and shows how this has led to male dominance over women and to male supremacy. Elizabeth Fisher ingeniously argued that the domestication of animals…led men to the idea of raping women. She claimed that the brutalization and violence connected with animal domestication led to men's sexual dominance and institutionalized aggression. More recently, Mary O'Brien built an elaborate explanation of the origin of male dominance on men's psychological need to compensate for their inability to bear children through the construction of institutions of dominance and, like Fisher, dated this "discovery" in the period of the discovery of animal domestication.[14]

The Marxist method

Marxist theory approaches the question of women's oppression quite differently—from a materialist standpoint. It is based not upon speculation, but upon piecing together what we actually know about the evolution of human society. Most importantly, we know that women have not always suffered oppression—in fact, the evidence shows that in a number of more primitive societies, women have been regarded as the equals of men. It was only recently in the evolution of human beings that the social position of women has fallen compared with that of men.

In his introduction to the first edition of *The Origin*, Engels explains materialism as follows:

> According to the materialist conception, the determining factor in history is, in the final instance, the production and reproduction of immediate life. This, again, is of a twofold character: on the one side, the production of the means of existence, of food, clothing and shelter and the tools necessary for that production; on the other side, the production of human beings themselves, the propagation of the species.[15]

But Marxism is both materialist and dialectical. It is based upon an understanding of history that sees human beings as both 1) products of the natural world and 2) able to interact with their natural surroundings, in the process changing themselves and the world around them.

It is true that there are some things about the earliest human societies that we cannot know because there are no written records. Nevertheless, by studying tools, bones, and other fossils, it is possible to see what distinguished our human ancestors from apes. In the first instance, it was their ability to plan their actions in order to gain greater control over nature. This enabled them to eke out a means of subsistence in a wider range of climates and circumstances—a process that Marx and Engels called labor. In his unfinished article, "The Part Played by Labor in the Transition from Ape to Man," Engels writes, "[I]n a sense, we have to say that labor created man himself."[16] Chris Harman has argued that apes

> are genetically programmed in narrow ways that provide them with the behavior appropriate to a limited range of en-

vironments, while we [humans] are characterized precisely by an immense flexibility in our behavior that enables us, virtually alone in the animal world, to thrive on any part of the globe. This is a fundamental difference between us and the existing apes. So gorillas are not to be found outside tropical rain forests, chimps outside wooded regions in sub-Saharan Africa, gibbons outside the tree tops of Southeast Asia, orangutans outside a few islands in Indonesia; by contrast, humans have been able to live across a vast swath of Africa, Europe and Asia for at least half a million years. Our genetic "specialty" is precisely that we are not specialized, not constrained by any limited range of instinctive behavior.[17]

The inclusion of meat in the diet meant that early humans could survive in a much wider variety of climates, so they could spread all over the world. The need for planning in hunting and other activities in turn necessitated coordination and verbal communication, which led to the development of the larynx. Toolmaking required manual dexterity and intelligence, which led to the development of the hand and the enlargement of the brain. The human anatomy thus evolved according to the "needs" of the labor process. But, in turn, the labor process advanced further still, according to the evolution of human anatomy—leading to improvements in the tools and other products used to master the environment and more complex forms of communication. As Engels put it, "Thus, the hand is not only the organ of labor, it is also the product of labor."[18] This same course of development applies to human society as a whole.

Primitive communism

Before class society, the idea of a strictly monogamous pairing of males and females with their offspring—the nuclear family—was unknown to human society. Inequality was also unknown. For more than two million years, humans lived in groups made up of people who were mostly related by blood, in conditions of relative equality. This understanding is an important part of Marxist theory, although much of the earliest evidence for it came from an unlikely source—seventeenth- and eighteenth-century Jesuit missionaries who recorded their observations of the Native American cultures they encountered.

The Jesuits mostly were appalled by the level of equality they found—including the sexual freedom and equality between women and men. One Jesuit, when he encountered the Montagnais-Naskapi of Eastern Canada, reported, "I told him that it was not honorable for a woman to love anyone else except her husband, and that, this evil being among them, he himself was not sure that his son, who was there present, was his son." But the Naskapi were equally appalled by the Jesuits. The man replied, "Thou hast no sense. You French people love only your own children; but we love all the children of our tribe."[19]

The Jesuits recorded their disbelief at the fact that the Indians neither had, nor apparently desired, any kind of social hierarchy. This comment from Father Paul Le Jeune, writing in 1634, again describing the Naskapi, is typical: They "cannot endure in the least those who seem desirous of assuming superiority over the others; they place all virtue in a certain gentleness or apathy."

Le Jeune and the other missionaries set out, of course, to change this state of affairs. "Alas," he complained, "if someone could stop the wanderings of the savages, and give authority to one of them to rule the others, we could see them converted and civilized in a short time." But the obstacles were many. "As they have neither political organization, nor offices, nor dignities, nor any authority, for they only obey their chief through good will toward him, therefore they never kill each other to acquire these honors. Also, as they are contented with a mere living, not one of them gives himself to the Devil to acquire wealth."[20]

Lewis Henry Morgan drew the conclusion, after spending a lengthy period living among the Iroquois in his native New York, that the kinship system used by the Iroquois traced all bloodlines through the mother rather than the father (matrilineal versus patrilineal descent). By studying other societies (initially other American Indian cultures), Morgan began to acquire evidence that human social organization had evolved, corresponding to changes in how people gained their livelihood. He outlined three distinct periods, each a progressive stage of social development. He called them "savagery, barbarism, and civilization," reflecting the terminology of the Victorian period. The names have changed since then, but the basic outline remains valid: the stage he called "savagery" refers to hunter-gatherer or foraging societies; "barbarism" is a stage in which agriculture predominated, first with "slash and burn" agriculture, or horticulture, and later using advanced techniques, such as the plow and large-scale irrigation; "civilization" is a term still used, which refers to the developments of urban society and the beginnings of industry.

Morgan's research helped support Marx and Engels' long-held contention that a long period of "primitive communism" preceded class society. But it also helped Engels to clarify precisely how women's oppression arose hand in hand with the rise of class society. Morgan's careful study of the Iroquois showed two things: 1) Iroquois women and men had a rigid division of labor between the sexes; but 2) women were the equals of men, with complete autonomy over their own responsibilities and decision-making power within society as a whole.[21]

Women elders participated in the deliberations of the decision-making council. As noted by a nineteenth-century observer: "They exercised a negative, or what we call a veto power, in the important question of the declaration of war. They had the right also to interpose in bringing about a peace." As Judith Brown notes, because women controlled the planting and cultivating, they were given a great deal of authority, even over men's activities:

It was not only in the domestic realm that the matrons controlled the dispensing of food. By supplying the essential provisions for male activities—the hunt, the warpath, and the Council—they were able to control these to some degree. Thus Randle writes, "Indirectly, too, it is stated that the women could hinder or actually prevent a war party which lacked their approval by not giving the supplies of dried corn and the moccasins which the warriors required."[22]

Thus, women's role in production afforded them—women elders in particular—considerable political power within society as a whole. Morgan's and others' data on the Iroquois stand alone in proving that women's oppression has not existed in all human societies. But it is worth noting that more recent research has provided a plethora of examples that show that women enjoyed relative equality with men in pre-class societies.[23]

For example, studies of !Kung bush people in the Kalahari Desert draw similar conclusions. Patricia Draper found that in !Kung hunter-gatherer societies, women contributed equally, if not more, to the food supply. She described the two sexes living in complete equality, noting:

Among the !Kung there is an extremely low level of cultural tolerance for aggressive behavior by anyone, male or female. In societies where aggressiveness and dominance are valued, these behaviors accrue disproportionately to males, and the females are common targets, resulting in the lowering of their status. !Kung women are not caught by this dimension of sex-role complementarity. They customarily maintain a mild manner, but so do their men.[24]

The rise of class society

Human evolution has taken place over a very long time—a period of millions of years. The earliest human ancestors (Homo habilus) probably appeared some two million or more years ago, while anatomically modern humans (Homo sapiens) did not appear until 100,000 to 200,000 years ago. The earliest forms of agriculture did not begin until 10,000 years ago, and it is only over the last thousand years that human society has experienced much more rapid technological development.[25]

For most of human history, it would have been impossible to accumulate wealth—nor was there much motivation to do so. For one thing, there would have been no place to store it. People lived first in nomadic bands—hunter-gatherer societies—sustaining themselves by some combination of gathering berries, roots, and other vegetable growth, and hunting or fishing. In most such societies, there would have been no point in working more than the several hours per day it takes to produce what is necessary for subsistence. But even among the first societies to advance to horticulture, it wasn't really possible to produce much more than what was to be immediately consumed by members of the band.

With the onset of more advanced agricultural production—through the use of the plow and/or advanced methods of irrigation—and the beginnings of settled communities, in some societies human beings were able to extract more than

the means of subsistence from the environment. This led to
the first accumulation of surplus, or wealth. As Engels argued
in *The Origin*: "Above all, we now meet the first iron plow-
share drawn by cattle, which made large-scale agriculture, the
cultivation of fields, possible and thus created a practically un-
restricted food supply in comparison with previous conditions."[26] This was a turning point for human society, for it
meant that, over time, production for use could be replaced
by production for exchange and eventually for profit—leading
to the rise of the first class societies some six thousand years
ago (first in Mesopotamia, followed a few hundred years later
by Egypt, Iran, the Indus Valley, and China).[27]

Engels argued that the rise of class society brought with
it rising inequality—between the rulers and the ruled, and
between men and women. At first the surplus was shared
with the entire clan—so wealth was not accumulated by any
one individual or groups of individuals. But gradually, as settled communities grew in size and became more complex social organizations, and, most importantly, as the surplus
grew, the distribution of wealth became unequal—and a
small number of men rose above the rest of the population in
wealth and power.

The sexual division of labor in class society

The crux of Engels' theory of women's oppression rests on
the relationship between the sexual division of labor and the
mode of production, which underwent a fundamental transfor-

mation with the onset of class society. In hunter-gatherer and horticultural societies, there was a sexual division of labor—rigidly defined sets of responsibilities for women and men. But both sexes were allowed a high degree of autonomy in performing those tasks. Moreover—and this is an element that has been learned since Engels' time—women not only provided much of the food for the band in hunter-gatherer societies, but also, in many cases, they provided most of the food.[28] So women in pre-class societies were able to combine motherhood and productive labor—in fact, there was no strict demarcation between the reproductive and productive spheres. Women, in many cases, could carry small children with them while they gathered or planted, or leave the children behind with other adults for a few hours at a time. Likewise, many goods could be produced in the household. Because women were central to production in these pre-class societies, systematic inequality between the sexes was nonexistent, and elder women in particular enjoyed relatively high status.

All that changed with the development of private property. According to the sexual division of labor, men tended to take charge of heavier agricultural jobs, like plowing, since it was more difficult for pregnant or nursing women and might endanger small children being carried along. Moreover, since men traditionally took care of big-game hunting (though not exclusively[29]), again, it made sense for them to oversee the domestication of cattle. Engels argued that the domestication of cattle preceded the use of the plow in agriculture, although it is now accepted that these two processes developed at the same time.[30] But this does not diminish the validity of his explanation as to why control over cattle fell to men.

As production shifted away from the household, the role of reproduction changed substantially. The shift toward agricultural production sharply increased the productivity of labor. This, in turn, increased the demand for labor—the greater the number of field workers, the higher the surplus. Thus, unlike hunter-gatherer societies, which sought to limit the number of offspring, agricultural societies sought to maximize women's reproductive potential, so the family would have more children to help out in the fields. Therefore, at the same time that men were playing an increasingly exclusive role in production, women were required to play a much more central role in reproduction.

The rigid sexual division of labor remained the same, but production shifted away from the household. The family no longer served anything but a reproductive function—as such, it became an economic unit of consumption. Women became trapped within their individual families, as the reproducers of society—cut off from production. These changes took place first among the property-owning families, the first ruling class. But eventually, the nuclear family became an economic unit of society as a whole.

It is important to understand that these changes did not

take place overnight, but over a period of thousands of years. Moreover, greed was not responsible, in the first instance, for the unequal distribution of wealth. Nor was male chauvinism the reason why power fell into the hands of (some) men, while the status of women fell dramatically. There is no evidence (nor any reason to assume) that women were coerced into this role by men. For property-owning families, a larger surplus would have been in the interest of all household members. Engels said of the first male "property owners" of domesticated cattle, "What is certain is that we must not think of him as a property owner in the modern sense of the word." He owned his cattle in the same sense that he owned the other tools required to obtain food and other necessities. But "the family did not multiply so rapidly as the cattle."[31] Agricultural output also increased sharply—some of which needed to be stored to feed the community in case of a poor harvest, and some of which could be traded for other goods.

Obviously, every society across the globe did not experience an identical succession of changes in the mode of production. Engels' personal knowledge was vast, but limited to Germany and classical Mediterranean and Asian societies. He relied primarily on Morgan's data to evaluate non-Eurasian societies. Nor do changes in the mode of production automatically lead to precise changes in reproduction. Thus, incest between brothers and sisters remained quite common in ancient Egypt, while it was banned in most comparably developed class societies. But since Engels' time, as Eleanor Burke Leacock maintains, "Archeological researches have yielded an undeniable picture of [hu]mankind's development from 'savage' hunters to 'barbarian' agriculturists and finally to 'civilizations' of the Ancient East."[32]

Likewise, Chris Harman writes, "[T]he exact route from hunter-gathering through horticulture and agriculture to civilization did vary considerably from one society to another." But,

> the divergent forms under which class society emerged must not make us forget the enormous similarities from society to society. Everywhere there was, in the beginning, primitive communism. Everywhere, once settled agricultural societies were formed, some lineages, lineage elders or "big men" could begin to gain prestige through their role in undertaking the redistribution of the little surplus that existed in the interests of the group as a whole. Everywhere, as the surplus grew, this small section of society came to control a greater share of the social wealth, putting it in a position where it could begin to crystallize out into a social class.[33]

The old communal forms of organization weren't transformed overnight, nor were they transformed uniformly from one society to the next. But they were transformed. The generosity inherent in primitive communist societies, in which the exchange of gifts is a central part of social life, changed qualitatively in conditions of inequality. Gift giving was traditionally a mutual exchange. But if the gift giver is wealthy while the receiver is without property, it is impossible for the receiver to reciprocate. In such conditions, the gift giver can easily become an exploiter or a tax collector. A chief who wields little or no authority in a foraging band can easily turn into a priest or a bureaucrat standing over the rest of society once classes emerge. And a man who owns a few head of cattle or a fertile patch of land can, under the right conditions, become a wealthy and powerful landlord.

Karen Sacks summarizes the impact of private property on women's overall standing in society:

> Private property transformed the relations between men and women within the household only because it also radically changed the political and economic relations in the larger *society*. For Engels the new wealth in domesticated animals meant that there was a surplus of goods available for exchange between productive units. With time, production by men specifically for exchange purposes developed, expanded, and came to overshadow the household's production for use... As production of exchange eclipsed production for use, it changed the nature of the household, the significance of women's work within it, and consequently women's position in society.[34]

The nuclear family: The root of women's oppression

It was under these circumstances that the monogamous nuclear family—the family as we know it—began to take form. The modern family arose for one purpose only: to pass on private property in the form of inheritance from one generation to the next. All the romantic imagery of "true love" that has since helped to idealize marriage in contemporary society can't change the fact that marriage is essentially a property relationship. Most people learn this all too clearly if they find themselves in divorce court.

From very early on, the nuclear family's material roots in class society were crystal clear to Marx and Engels. In 1846, they argued in the *German Ideology* that with the abolition of private property, "the abolition of the family is self-evident."[35] Engels understood the hypocrisy of contemporary ruling-class marriage and the degradation of women that went with it. In *The Origin*, he describes ruling-class marriage as typically, "a conjugal partnership of leaden boredom, known as 'domestic bliss.'"[36] But, crucially, Engels also traced the historical rise of the family as a property relationship—which developed hand in hand with class society. He demonstrated this relationship by showing the meaning of the term "family" in the Roman Empire:

> The original meaning of the word "family" (familia) is not the compound of sentimentality and domestic strife which forms the ideal of the present-day philistine; among the Romans it did not at first even refer to the married pair and their children but only to the slaves. Famulus means domestic slave, and *familia* is the total number of slaves belonging to one man. As late as the time of Gaius, the familia, id est patrimonium (family, that is the patrimony, the inheritance) was bequeathed by will. The term was invented by the Romans to denote a new social organism whose head ruled over wife and children and a number of slaves, and was invested under Roman paternal power with rights of life and death over them all.[37]

Engels adds, quoting Marx, "The modern family contains in germ not only slavery (servitus) but also serfdom, since from the beginning it is related to agricultural services. It contains in miniature all the contradictions which later extend throughout society and its state."[38]

But there was a further contradiction between earlier communal social organization and rising class society, Engels argues. Wealth was owned by men, but since most societies were matrilineal, inheritance was passed through the mother, not the father. Moreover, without strict monogamy, a man cannot be certain that his wife's children are also his own. Engels writes,

> Thus, on the one hand, in proportion as wealth increased it made the man's position in the family more important than the woman's, and on the other hand created an impulse to exploit this strengthened position in order to overthrow, in favor of his children, the traditional order of inheritance.... Mother right, therefore, had to be overthrown, and overthrown it was.[39]

Engels notes that because this transformation of the family took place in prehistoric times, we can't know how and when it happened. However, "that it did take place is more than sufficiently proved by the abundant traces of mother right which have been collected."[40] Engels probably overstates this point. It is true that the societies he (and Morgan) analyzed tended to be matrilineal. But the Iroquois was a relatively advanced horticultural society. Engels wrongly concluded that, according to the theory of evolution, this necessarily meant that all the earliest hunter-gatherer societies were matrilineal. There is no way to prove or disprove this assertion, precisely because there are no written records. Although it can reasonably be assumed that some early human societies were matrilineal, we cannot assume that they all organized kinship structures in this way.[41]

But whether or not all early societies were matrilineal is not as important as it might seem. What is indisputable is that the onset of class society brought with it a universal shift toward patrilineage—and, more importantly, the role of men as "heads" of their households. Engels was undoubtedly correct—with more supporting evidence today than when he was writing—that the rise of the nuclear family brought with it a degradation of women that was unknown in pre-class societies. Engels argued,

> The overthrow of mother right was the world historic defeat of the female sex. The man took command in the home also; the woman was degraded and reduced to servitude; she became the slave of his lust and a mere instrument for the production of children. . . . In order to make certain of the wife's fidelity and therefore the paternity of his children, she is delivered over unconditionally into the power of the husband; if he kills her, he is only exercising his rights.[42]

That the rise of the family was a consequence—and not a cause, as some feminists argue—of the rise of classes is central to Engels' argument. Eleanor Burke Leacock describes how the rise of the modern family developed in response to the needs of a rising class society:

> The separation of the family from the clan and the institution of monogamous marriage were the social expressions of

developing private property; so-called monogamy afforded the means through which property could be individually inherited. And private property for some meant no property for others, or the emerging of differing relations to production on the part of different social groups. The core of Engels' formulation lies in the intimate connection between the emergence of the family as an economic unit dominated by the male and this development of classes.[43]

Moreover, Engels puts forward a convincing explanation as to why women ended up the oppressed sex, rather than men. Many writers who accept Engels' analysis of the rise of the nuclear family have nevertheless argued that it does not explain gender inequality. This has led to a search for a specific explanation—in particular, in men's role in warfare or trade. But as Coontz and Henderson note,

> The existence of separate sexual spheres can certainly lead to male dominance if the male sphere expands at the expense of the female, but most recorded instances of such a disruption—from warfare, migration, trade, or cultural stress—are the result of contact with already unequal and aggressive societies.[44]

Engels' analysis is straightforward—it may need further development, but its essence is there, plain to see. The sexual division of labor that existed in pre-class societies, when production for use was the dominant mode of production, carried no implication of gender inequality. Women were able to combine their reproductive and productive roles, so both sexes were able to perform productive labor. But with the rise of class society, when production for exchange began to dominate, the sexual division of labor helped to erode equality between the sexes. Production and trade increasingly occurred away from the household, so that the household became a sphere primarily for reproduction. As Coontz and Henderson argue,

> The increasing need for redistribution (both within local groups and between them) and the political tasks this creates have consequences for sex roles in that these political roles are often filled by males, even in matrilineal/matrilocal societies. Presumably this flows from the division of labor that associates males with long-distance activities, external affairs, and products requiring group-wide distribution, while females are more occupied with daily productive tasks from which they cannot be absented.[45]

Hence, the beginnings of a "public" versus a "private" sphere, with women increasingly trapped in the household in property-owning families. The rise of the family itself explains women's subordinate role within it. For the first time in human history, women's ability to give birth kept them from playing a significant part in production.

Enforced monogamy and prostitution: Two sides of the same coin

Engels makes it clear that the development of a family based upon strict monogamy has nothing to do with morality: "Marriage according to the bourgeois conception was a contract, a legal transaction, and the most important one of all because it disposed of two human beings, body and mind, for life." He quips,

> And if strict monogamy is the height of all virtue, then the palm must go to the tapeworm, which has a complete set of male and female sexual organs in each of its 50 to 200 proglottides or sections, and spends its whole life copulating in all its sections with itself.[46]

Moreover, he argues, the monogamous family ideal is based upon a fundamental hypocrisy. From its very beginning, the family has been stamped "with its specific character of monogamy for the woman only, but not for the man." In the classic patriarchal families of Rome or Greece, men were legally polygamous. And even after polygamy was legally abolished in most societies, men continued to enjoy greater sexual freedom. Acts of infidelity on the part of women, which Victorian society condemned in Engels' time (and for which contemporary capitalist society still holds a double standard), are "considered honorable in a man, or, at the worst, a slight moral blemish which he cheerfully bears." Thus, he concludes of monogamous marriage:

> It was not in any way the fruit of individual sex love, with which it had nothing whatever to do; marriages remained as before marriages of convenience. It was the first form of the family to be based not on natural but on economic conditions—on the victory of private property over primitive, natural communal property.[47]

Even then, the requirements of monogamous marriage have been in most societies more an ideal than a reality, even for women. Though men and women are legally equally bound to practice strict monogamy, with a wink and a nod, both sexes not uncommonly violate this obligation. Again, infidelity among men is more acceptable—indeed, to this day, the prevailing ideology is that men are "naturally" inclined to desire multiple sex partners while women's biology makes them more content with just one. Nevertheless, as Engels observed, with the rise of the family, "adultery became an unavoidable social institution—denounced, severely penalized, but impossible to suppress."[48]

Engels argues that the frequency of sex between married men and unmarried women became institutionalized over time. It "flourishes in the most varied forms throughout the whole period of civilization and develops more and more into open prostitution." Thus, side by side with the development of monogamous marriage grew the first commodification of sex in the form of prostitution—both products of class society. "With the rise of the inequality of property," he argues, "wage labor appears...and at the same time, as its necessary correlate, the professional prostitution of free women side by side with the forced surrender of the slave." Monogamy and prostitution are two sides of the same coin, or, in Engels' words, "monogamy and prostitution are indeed contradictions, but inseparable contradictions, poles of the same state of society."[49] This observation by Engels is extremely insightful, for he could probably not have imagined, living in nineteenth-century Victorian England, the degree to which the sexual commodification of women would turn into a massive and highly profitable industry in this century.

The family under capitalism

Engels no doubt would also have marveled at other ways in which advanced capitalism has made dramatic changes in women's lives over the last century. Today, most women hold jobs outside the home. In the United States, women make up more than half the workforce. Moreover, technology has advanced so that the time spent on household chores, like laundry, has been reduced to a fraction of what it was in Engels' time. Fast-food restaurants make it possible for women to spend less time cooking. Public schooling means that the time women spend on childrearing is greatly reduced from the days when they barely left the home.

Yet, despite all these changes, women are still oppressed. Women's wages are substantially lower than men's throughout the world. Sexual harassment is a common problem for women workers. Substantial numbers of women still suffer from rape and domestic violence. Massive profits are made each year, not only from pornography, but through the sexual objectification of women in advertising and throughout the mass media. And, although most women hold jobs outside the home, society still holds them responsible for the bulk of childrearing and housework.[50]

And the fundamentals of Engels' analysis of women's oppression still hold. He locates the source of women's oppression as stemming primarily from their reproductive role within the family and the family's role as an economic unit in society:

> In the old communistic household, which comprised many couples and their children, the task entrusted to women of managing the household was as much a public, a socially necessary industry as the procuring of food by the men. With the patriarchal family and still more with the single monogamous family, a change came. Household management lost its public character. It no longer concerned society. It became a private service; the wife became the head servant, excluded from all participation in social production. Not until the coming of modern large-scale industry was the road to social production opened to her again—and then, only to the proletarian wife. But it was opened in such a manner that, if she carries out her duties in the private service of her family, she remains excluded from public production and unable to earn; and if she wants to take part in public production and earn independently, she cannot carry out family duties.... The modern individual family is founded on the open or concealed domestic slavery of the wife, and modern society is a mass composed of these individual families as its molecules.[51]

To be sure, Engels' analysis needs some updating. For one thing, as the preceding passage shows, he underestimated the extent to which middle- and even ruling-class women would enter the professional and managerial workforce in this century, while a staff of servants relieves them of most domestic tasks. More importantly from a theoretical standpoint, Engels' analysis of the family focused almost exclusively on the role of the ruling-class family. Thus, he never fully anticipated the degree to which capitalism would manage to incorporate working-class women into the labor force without diminishing their centrality to the reproduction of labor power. This is certainly understandable, since women in their childbearing years only began to enter the workforce on a mass scale with the development of reliable birth control in the twentieth century. Engels also held an almost romantic vision of the proletarian household:

> Here there is no property, for the preservation and inheritance of which monogamy and male supremacy were established; hence there is no incentive to make this male supremacy effective. What is more, there are no means of making it so. Bourgeois law, which protects this supremacy, exists only for the possessing class and their dealings with the proletarians.... And now that large-scale industry has taken the wife out of the home onto the labor market and into the factory.... no basis for any kind of male supremacy is left in the proletarian household, except, perhaps, for something of the brutality toward women that has spread since the introduction of monogamy (emphasis added).[52]

Here, Engels rightly argues that working-class women's entry into production is a step forward. But he overestimates the degree to which this alone impacts the status of women to men within the working class. From this passage, it is clear that Engels recognizes, but downplays, the impact of ideology on society as a whole. But as Martha Gimenez argues, "The class that controls the means of production also controls the conditions for the physical and social reproduction of the propertyless classes and sets the parameters within which the empirically observable forms of sexual inequality develop and change."[53] If anything, the oppression experienced by working-class women is much more severe than that of wealthy women, precisely because their families have no property. (This was undoubtedly also true in Engels' day.) There is no comparison between the life experiences of ruling-class women like Hillary Clinton or Ivana Trump and those of a woman clerical or factory worker.

But the difference is not only one of degree. As Engels described, once production shifted away from the household, the role of the family increasingly became one of privatized reproduction. Under capitalism, despite all the other changes that have taken place, the nuclear family remains a center for privatized reproduction. But ruling-class families exist to reproduce the next ruling class; working-class families reproduce the next generation of workers. The very nature of the oppression suffered by women of different classes is therefore quite different. Historically, ruling-class women tend to be little more than showpieces, whose main social contribution is the birth of a son to inherit the family's wealth. Boredom and a sense of uselessness traditionally characterize ruling-class women's oppression. When they enter the managerial or professional workforce, this does not in any way increase their oppression as women, since they have a staff of servants at their disposal.

The same can't be said for working-class women. Despite

public education, today's capitalists still take precious little responsibility for the legion of workers whose labor produces their profits. The fact that in the United States today forty-four million people have no health care is one example of this lack of responsibility. The burden for the reproduction of labor power still lies primarily within the working-class family—and women's role within it—both for enabling today's generation of workers to replenish themselves so they can return to their jobs each day and for rearing the next generation of workers through childhood. The working-class family is extremely valuable to the capitalist system as a cheap means of reproducing labor power.

The large-scale entry of working-class women into the labor force hasn't changed that fact. Engels argued that working-class women who hold jobs are nevertheless also expected to fulfill their family duties. But while Engels implied that working women would have to make a choice between the two roles, the experience of advanced capitalism has proven otherwise. Working-class women are expected to do both. The result is that working-class women face a double burden, in which they return home from work at the end of the day only to face all their family responsibilities. Each day is a never-ending battle to fulfill both sets of responsibilities.[54] Thus, although women play a productive role in advanced capitalism, this alone hasn't translated into equality with men as it did in pre-class societies. As long as privatized reproduction within the nuclear family continues, so will women's oppression.

Women's liberation and socialism

Given the relationship of the working-class family to the capitalist system, the answer is therefore not, as some feminists have suggested, convincing men to take on a greater share of housework. While socialists are in favor of men sharing housework, we hold none of the feminist illusions that this is a solution to women's oppression, for reproduction would continue to be privatized. This solution is effectively one that would only affect working-class families. It would have virtually no effect on any family with the means to hire domestic labor. It would mean, however, that working-class men would share the burden for the reproduction of labor power along with working-class women—to the continued benefit of the capitalist class. Both working-class women *and* men deserve more, not less, leisure time—particularly today, when U.S. workers on average are working a month longer per year than they did thirty years ago.[55] Martha Gimenez argues,

> [C]hanges in the division of labor between the sexes (i.e., greater male participation in domestic work and childcare) which seem to be "progressive" and useful for changing sex role stereotypes, are not only a relatively inefficient form of time use (hence the preference for purchasing domestic labor in the market by those who can afford it) but what is more important, also contribute to strengthen the family as

the major locus for the reproduction of labor power, daily and generationally.[56]

Nor is legal reform the solution. Again, socialists support legislative reforms, such as an equal rights amendment, which would make women legally the equals of men. But, as Engels argued, "The legal inequality of [men and women]...is not the cause but the effect of the economic oppression of the woman." If an equal rights amendment passed through Congress tomorrow, it would make virtually no difference in the day-to-day lives of working-class women. Nevertheless, socialists favor legal reform because of the changes in consciousness that it can produce. Engels argues, "the necessity of creating real social equality" between women and men

> will only be seen in the clear light of day when both possess legally complete equality of rights. Then it will be plain that the first condition for the liberation of the wife is to bring the whole female sex back into public industry, and that this in turn demands that the characteristic of the monogamous family as the economic unit of society be abolished.[57]

Winning legal equality for women can help to make it clearer that women's oppression can only be ended when the relations of production on which it is based are overthrown. What was true in Engels' time is even more true today—society has more than enough wealth to turn housework and the more burdensome aspects of childrearing into a "social industry"— into paid, productive labor. But this can't happen as long as production exists only for profit. Nothing short of a socialist transformation of society will win genuine equality for women:

> With the transfer of the means of production into common ownership, the single family ceases to be the economic unit of society. Private housekeeping is transformed into a social industry. The care and education of the children becomes a public affair; society looks after all children alike, whether they are legitimate or not.... Will not that suffice to bring about the gradual growth of unconstrained sexual intercourse and with it a more tolerant public opinion in regard to a maiden's honor and a woman's shame? And finally.... [C]an prostitution disappear without dragging monogamy with it into the abyss?[58]

Was Engels right?

Engels has many critics. Some of this criticism has been invaluable. In particular, the anthropologists Eleanor Burke Leacock and Karen Sacks have applied more recent data to help further develop the Marxist approach to women's oppression as laid out by Engels in *The Origin*, while casting aside his assertions that have been disproved. Stephanie Coontz and Peta Henderson have developed a useful analysis of the rise of patrilineal descent, which builds upon Engels' work. More recently, Chris Harman has developed a critique of Engels that helps to clarify his insights. All have been cited above.

One mistake that some of Engels' critics make, however—and this is especially, though not exclusively, true of academics—is to dwell so much on the particulars as to obscure the theoretical framework developed by Engels. When one examines every detail of each and every tree, it is all too easy to miss the forest. For example, the sociologist Martha Gimenez, in an essay also cited above, offers some valid criticism of specific assertions made by Engels and, for all intents and purposes, convincingly defends the essence of Marxist theory. Yet she argues that "the presence of Marxist and non-Marxist elements in Engels' text is an important determinant of the ambiguous nature of his views"—as if somehow Marx and Engels had parted ways.[59] Engels may have made a number of errors, but this was not one of them.

The problem is made worse when those who are unsympathetic to Marxism are doing the dissecting. Many feminist writers accuse Marx and Engels of "economic reductionism"—of reducing all social questions, including women's oppression, to class relations. The accusation usually rests on the false assumption that Marxism subordinates women's oppression to the more important arena of the class struggle. The underlying assumption is, of course, that the root of women's oppression is at least partly personal in nature, and unrelated to class society—a product purely of the unequal personal relationships between women and men. Eleanor Leacock makes the point, "In western academic circles secondhand knowledge of (or assumptions about) Marxist ideas are legion, but Marx's and Engels' works are all too seldom read. The usual practice is to set up Marxist theory as the straw man of economic determinism and then to knock it down."[60]

One of those most hostile to Marxism, Catherine MacKinnon, writes in her anti-Marxist diatribe, *Toward a Feminist Theory of the State*, that Marx was interested in women's oppression "only in passing." She accuses Engels of sexism explicitly, stating, "The key dynamic assumption in Engels' analysis of women's situation, that without which Engels' history does not move is (in a word) sexism." Thus, she concludes, "The classical socialists believed first socialism, then women's liberation," as if Marx and Engels swept women's liberation under the rug.[61] MacKinnon never bothers to present documentation of these charges. Her own analysis locates the source of women's oppression in the existence of pornography. And she regards the criminalization of pornography as a step toward ending women's oppression—a right-wing conclusion that a broad range of feminists have rejected.

Nevertheless, even many feminists who have attempted to incorporate questions of class share a similar assumption about Marxism. Thus, Gerda Lerner criticizes what she describes as "the insistence of Marxists that questions of sex relations must be subordinated to questions of class relations."[62]

In particular, the feminist argument often goes, Marxism cannot (and does not seek to) explain the more personal aspects of women's oppression because it locates the root of women's oppression in class society. This is a caricature of Marxism, which assumes that Marxists only concern themselves with exploitation at the workplace. In reality, Marxists do not "rank" oppressions. But locating the economic roots of inequality is precisely the way to understand how seemingly quite different forms of oppression have come to play a crucial—and often interdependent—role in propping up the system of exploitation.

Far from ignoring the personal aspects of women's oppression, Engels laid out for the first time the theoretical framework for understanding them. This should be obvious to anyone who has made the effort to read *The Origin* with an open mind. Engels incorporated into his analysis all aspects of women's oppression—including domestic abuse, the alienation of sexuality, the commodification of sex, the drudgery of housework, and the hypocrisy of enforced monogamy. And most importantly, he emphasized the inequality between women and men within the family. Moreover, he did so in the Victorian era, when such ideas were far less commonplace than they are today in the aftermath of the women's liberation movement. Locating the source of women's oppression in class society in no way limits our understanding of the impact that it has had on the lives of individual women.

It should not be surprising that there are a fair number of errors in *The Origin*—if only because Engels was so far ahead of his time. The most important errors made by Engels, in fact, are those instances in which he accepts certain aspects of Victorian morality. Thus, after a scathing attack on enforced monogamy, he nevertheless guesses that socialism will bring with it a flowering of...*monogamy,* in the form of "individual sex love." There is, of course, no way to predict what sort of relationships people will choose in a society in which sexuality is no longer alienated. Given the extent of sexual alienation present in today's society, it is difficult even to imagine. Moreover, any analysis of gay oppression is entirely absent from Engels' analysis, even though more recent Marxist theory has pinpointed the roots of gay oppression, like women's, in the rise of the nuclear family.

Nevertheless, as the following passage makes clear, Engels' method not only opened the door to understanding women's oppression, but also put forward a vision of women's liberation, which has continued both to inform and inspire successive generations of socialists since his time:

> What we can now conjecture about the way in which sexual relations will be ordered after the impending overthrow of capitalist production is mainly of a negative character, limited for the most part to what will disappear. But what will there be new? That will be answered when a new generation has grown up: a generation of men who never in their lives have known what it is to buy a woman's surrender with money or any other social instrument of power; a generation of women who have never known what it is to give themselves to a man from any other considerations than real love or to refuse to give themselves to their lover from fear of the economic consequences. When these people are in the world, they will care precious little what anybody today thinks they ought to do; they will make their own practice and their corresponding public opinion about the practice of each individual—and that will be the end of it.[63]

CHAPTER 2

Abortion Rights:
The Socialist Case

ONE IN every three women in the United States has an abortion before the age of forty-five, according to the Alan Guttmacher Institute.[1] So most women today have either had abortions themselves or know someone who has needed one. Many older women remember the days when abortion was illegal. It should be no surprise, therefore, that a majority of the population continues to oppose overturning the Supreme Court's 1973 *Roe v. Wade* decision that made abortion legal, despite the ideological gains made by opponents of abortion in recent years.[2]

Whether or not abortion is a legal right, women desperate to terminate an unwanted pregnancy continue to have them—even if it means self-inflicting abortions or seeking out illegal back-alley abortionists. Worldwide, twenty-six million legal abortions are performed every year, while another twenty million are illegally performed in countries where abortion is severely restricted or banned.[3] In the late 1940s through the early 1950s, when abortion was banned in the United States, up to 1.3 million illegal abortions were performed each year, according to experts.[4]

Illegal abortions are expensive and humiliating for women—often performed without anesthesia and in dark and unsanitary conditions. But most important, illegal abortions are extremely dangerous. Women desperate to end a pregnancy use harsh chemicals or coat hangers to attempt a self-inflicted abortion. Back-alley abortions often result in massive hemorrhaging and infection, while women delay medical treatment for fear of criminal charges. Large numbers of women die when abortion is illegal. According to the World Health Organization, seventy-eight thousand women around the world die from unsafe abortions every year.[5]

The death toll during the century when abortion was illegal in the United States is unknown, but the number is certainly large—some estimates are as high as 10,000 each year. A University of Colorado study done in the late 1950s reported that 350,000 women experienced postoperative complications each year from illegal abortions in the United States.[6]

These conditions explain why legal abortion is essential to women's rights—and why the women's liberation movement fought so hard to win this right in the 1960s and 1970s, while millions more have fought to preserve it since it has been under attack. The April 25, 2004, March for Women's Lives drew more than a million supporters of choice to Washington, D.C., making it clear that the right to choose remains crucial for women from all walks of life.

The right to choose to end an unwanted pregnancy is central to women's control over their own bodies and reproductive lives. No one else should have this control—not the church, state, husband, parents, or boyfriend. The reason is simple: Women must bear the emotional and physical trauma—and ultimately the financial burden—of carrying an unwanted pregnancy to term.

The right to choose whether or when to bear a child is particularly important for women today, since a majority of women of childbearing age are part of the workforce. Women, whether or not they work outside the home, bear the bulk of responsibility for raising children into adulthood. Child care costs for infants and preschoolers often run as high as state college tuition. Single mothers bear full responsibility for their children, at wages much lower than men's. It is no coincidence that most abortions today occur among never-married women and women living with a male partner to whom they are not married.[7]

Women's right to abortion is therefore a precondition for women's equality. Unless women can end an unwanted pregnancy they cannot be the equals of men in society. That is why abortion was a key demand of the women's liberation movement of the late 1960s and remains a center of struggle for women's rights today.

Class, race, and reproductive freedom

But the right to abortion is just one aspect of a much larger issue of reproductive rights. Although in recent decades the battle has centered around preserving the legal right to abortion, reproductive freedom includes more than the legal right to terminate an unwanted pregnancy.

Winning reproductive freedom entails a fight for the abortion rights of poor and working-class women. Even when abortion is illegal, wealthy women have—and have always had—the money and private doctors to obtain abortions, while poor women face the choice of carrying an unwanted pregnancy to term or risking their lives in an unsafe, illegal abortion. Because of the economic consequences of racial discrimination, the lives of Black women and Latinas are most at risk when abortion is illegal.

Before 1970, when abortion was made legal in New York City, Black women made up 50 percent of all women who died after an illegal abortion, while Puerto Rican women were 44 percent.[8]

"Women who have abortions are predominantly young, single, from minority groups and low income," according to the Alan Guttmacher Institute and Physicians for Reproductive Choice and Health.[9] Low-income women need access to abortion, financially out of reach for so many, as a basic part of health care coverage. Teenagers, who are the most vulnerable to the consequences of an unwanted pregnancy, deserve unfettered and affordable access to birth control and abortion.

The fight for reproductive rights is also a fight for those who wish to have children but are denied that right. Lesbian and gay couples should have the right to raise children as same-sex parents, with the full legal and financial benefits of marriage. Black and Brown women the world over deserve the right to choose to have children in the face of racist "population control" programs.

The argument for population control has been the excuse to justify involuntary sterilizations on a massive scale, and coercive and abusive methods on the part of birth control programs—both inside and outside U.S. borders. Such programs targeted African Americans, Native Americans, and disabled people in the United States throughout much of the twentieth century, and continue to target Black and Brown people in poor countries around the world today.

The politics of modern population control programs reflect the deep racism of those who own and control the world's wealth. The first population control programs were heavily influenced by eugenics, the "science" of "improving heredity"—in the image of white Anglo-Saxons. Margaret Sanger, a founder of Planned Parenthood and an early pioneer in the fight for birth control, abandoned earlier arguments for women's rights and replaced them with eugenicist arguments as she sought allies in the ruling class to fund her projects. In 1919, her publication, *Birth Control Review,* stated, "More children from the fit and less from the unfit— that is the chief issue of birth control."[10]

Those "unfit" to bear children, according to the eugenicists, included the mentally and physically disabled, prisoners, and the non-white poor. Racist population control policies left large numbers of Black women, Latinas, and Native American women sterilized against their will or without their knowledge. In 1974, an Alabama court found that between 100,000 and 150,000 poor Black teenagers were sterilized each year in Alabama. A 1970s study showed 25 percent of Native American women had been sterilized, and that Black and Latina married women had been sterilized in much greater proportions than married women in the population at large.[11]

After the Second World War, the U.S. government began targeting poor countries where it had economic interests for population control programs. In 1967, Congress allocated some $35 million to the U.S. Agency for International Development (USAID) specifically for population control in poor countries around the world. In the 1960s, the International Planned Parenthood Foundation, using U.S. government money, played a key role in a coercive sterilization program in Puerto Rico. By 1968, one-third of women of childbearing age in Puerto Rico—still a U.S. colony—had been permanently sterilized. Many of these women were sterilized without their clear consent, or without telling them the operation was permanent.[12]

While in recent years population control programs have steered clear of admitting blatantly racist policies, in practice they are just as racist as the early eugenicists' programs. Today, programs encouraging sterilization continue to target Black and Brown women and men in poor countries around the world in the name of population control.[13]

And inside the U.S., since the 1970s, while Medicaid funding for abortion and contraception is all but unavailable for poor women, Medicaid continues to cover over 90 percent of sterilization costs—a more than subtle means of coercion.

These are the reasons why reproductive freedom—the right to choose whether and when to have children—is not just a women's issue. It is also a class issue, a racial issue, and an issue of global justice.

The anti-abortion crusade: Political, not moral

Right-wing organizations, with names such as the Moral Majority, are neither morally superior, nor are they anywhere near the majority. They represent an extremely well-funded minority—with allies in high places, like Congress and the White House. To be sure, these right-wingers couch their opposition with pious phrases praising "the sanctity of life" and the "sanctity of marriage."

But they are hypocrites. Newt Gingrich, for example—a leading spokesperson for the sanctity of marriage—is now on his third marriage. This crusade is political, not moral.

Morality is personal. Those who oppose abortion should be able to follow their own consciences—and at the same time allow other people to follow theirs. No one in the pro-choice movement has ever suggested that anyone personally opposed to abortion should be forced to have one. Yet the goal of the anti-abortion crusade is to impose—by law—a very conservative set of moral values on the rest of the population.

Therefore, it is inaccurate to frame the abortion debate as a moral argument over whether human life begins at the moment of conception. There is no general agreement among different religious faiths as to when human life begins, nor is there evidence that the Bible prohibits abortion.[14] Opinions about abortion vary from one religion to the next, and have changed over time.

While the Catholic Church, along with various Protestant fundamentalist organizations, are prominent in the anti-abortion movement, forty-five other religious organizations are actively pro-choice. As early as 1962, the United Presbyterian Church began calling for abortion law reform, followed by the American Lutheran Church Executive Committee in 1963 and the Unitarian Universalist Association in 1964. After New York made abortion legal in 1971, the Clergy Consultation Service, an organization of 1,200 Protestant ministers and Jewish rabbis, set up abortion referral services in twenty states. The service helped many thousands of women travel to New York to obtain abortions before the *Roe v. Wade* decision in 1973.[15]

In fact, the Catholic Church itself has not always opposed early abortion. Until the mid–nineteenth century, the Church (along with the rest of society) had no sanctions against abortion through roughly the fourth month of pregnancy. It wasn't until 1869, when Pope Pius IX reworked the teaching on abortion, when the Church first demanded excommunication for anyone who aborted a pregnancy.[16] It is also worth noting that, however vehement Church leaders have been in condemning contraception and abortion, opinion polls and surveys consistently show that their advice has gone unheeded by the Catholic population, who practice birth control and abortion at roughly the same rates as the rest of the U.S. population.

By the end of the 1960s, the Church, already organizing opposition to artificial birth control, began turning its attention to abortion. From the time of the Supreme Court's decision in 1973 until 1976, the Catholic Church formed the core of the gathering anti-abortion offensive. Besides providing the National Right to Life Committee with the bulk of its funding, the National Conference of Catholic Bishops organized an anti-abortion group in every congressional district across the United States.[17]

The bigoted roots of the Christian Right

No sooner was abortion made legal in the United States in 1973 than right-wing lawmakers and organizations set out to overturn it. But the 1980 election of anti-abortion President Ronald Reagan helped to propel opposition to abortion into the political mainstream. No longer simply an arm of the Catholic Church, the anti-abortion crusade emerged as central to the platform of a loose coalition known as the "New Right." Today's Christian Right has its origins in the New Right—which did not even pretend to be religiously motivated, but brought together a variety of religious and political organizations ranging from Reverend Jerry Falwell's Moral Majority to the National Conservative Caucus.

The agenda of the New Right should dispel any myth that it believed in the sanctity of human life: It included support for the death penalty, support for nuclear weapons, and massive social spending cuts for the poor. Between fiscal years 1982 and 1985, for example, Congress cut $5 billion from school lunch, breakfast, and summer food programs for poor children. California Republican Rep. Robert K. Dornan even sponsored the Human Life Amendment—that would ban abortion under all circumstances, not just for rape and incest victims, but even if the woman would die if she gave birth. So much for respecting *human* life.[18]

In reality, the New Right was formed to oppose all the gains made by the social movements of the 1960s—not just the women's movement, but the Black Power and gay liberation movements. On this basis, the New Right united Protestant fundamentalists with old-time segregationists and other bigots to launch an ambitious campaign that shifted the political climate rightward during the 1980s. This pressure succeeded in gaining Republican Party support for passage of the Human Life Amendment and a plank calling for appointment of federal judges opposed to abortion.

The New Right opposed all aspects of equal rights for women, along with sex education in schools. Its opposition to abortion was impossible to separate from its desire to return women to their traditional role within the nuclear family—as wives and mothers, and nothing more. In the 1980s, the hallmark of the New Right was not merely opposition to abortion, but also to the Equal Rights Amendment (ERA), a Constitutional amendment that would have established women's basic equality with men. Phyllis Schlafly's Stop ERA organization campaigned as ardently against the ERA as the National Right to Life Committee campaigned against abortion.

The leaders of the Christian Right believed that the increasing numbers of women in the labor force, especially married women of childbearing age, were undermining the nuclear family. The women's liberation movement, which fought for abortion rights and passage of the ERA, was to blame. To this day, these right-wingers oppose all aspects of women's rights, and believe that the growing numbers of women in the workforce—along with abortion—are undermining the "traditional" nuclear family.

It could reasonably be argued that the "traditional family" ideal—the breadwinning husband and stay-at-home mom—

never actually existed, since many working-class women have always worked outside the home. But this ideal—of the "Ozzie and Harriet" and "Leave it to Beaver" variety—was a centerpiece of the segregated and reactionary era of the 1950s. And that is exactly the era to which the forces of the Christian Right want to return.

The link between the Christian Right's opposition to abortion and the bigotry of this bygone era was perhaps most transparent at Republican Senator Strom Thurmond's (now deceased) December 9, 2002, birthday celebration, where Republican Senator Trent Lott—who fights daily to carry out the Christian Right's agenda in Congress—praised Thurmond's 1948 presidential campaign, whose centerpiece was opposition to integration.

"We're proud of it. And if the rest of the country had followed our lead, we wouldn't have had all these problems over all these years either," Lott said.[19]

The Christian Right's opposition to abortion has its basis in this context. Its "pro-family" agenda attacks all of the gains made by the social movements of the 1960s. Its leaders' virulent opposition to women's liberation is matched by their hostility to affirmative action and gay rights.

In the 1990s, the Christian Right supported Clinton's so-called welfare reform that threw millions of poor families, women, and children into deeper poverty, and pushed for teen abstinence programs. Today, the Christian Right is not only behind Bush's support for a gay marriage ban and his attacks on abortion, but also his $1.5 billion program to promote marriage specifically in poor Black areas, where it believes the traditional family is most "threatened" by single motherhood.

Since its inception, the anti-abortion movement has been made up of dedicated activists, but their confidence grew in the 1980s, with Ronald Reagan in the White House. Anti-abortion activists from organizations such as Operation Rescue began appearing outside of abortion clinics in every major city in the 1980s, harassing and antagonizing women exercising their legal right to choose, and condemning them as murderers. Though the anti-abortion movement became marginalized during the Clinton years in the 1990s, its core of crusaders continued to combine activism with its legal strategy to undermine the right to choose. As Operation Rescue leader Randall Terry announced in 1989, "We are launching a two-pronged offensive. Thousands will surround abortion mills to rescue children and mothers, and we will impact state legislatures with equal force."[20]

Anti-abortion zealots continued to organize rallies and anti-abortion protests to hold together a network of activists—arguing that blockading abortion clinics was in the tradition of the civil rights movement. Secondly, on the political front, they aimed their sights on whittling away at the legal right to abortion, by fighting to impose legal restrictions and other obstacles on women's right to decide to terminate an unwanted pregnancy.

After nearly three decades of unrelenting attacks from the Right, these forces have done much to reshape mainstream arguments about abortion rights. From the 1976 Hyde Amendment denying abortion funding to poor Medicaid recipients to the more recent bans on so-called partial birth abortions, each new restriction has further eroded women's access to abortion.

In addition, each restriction has led further and further away from the ideas of women's rights: most centrally, the idea that women should have the right to control their own bodies. All of the anti-abortion arguments assume that women's bodies should be subject to control by others, be it parents, spouse, boyfriend, or government restrictions—because women choose abortion for "frivolous reasons" and "selfishly" delay their abortions for the sake of convenience. As one abortion opponent wrote in the *Arkansas Gazette,* "Can we really trade a life for the risk of stretch marks?"[21]

The 1990s: How abortion rights were eroded under a pro-choice president

But if the anti-abortion crusade maintained its activist focus during the Clinton years, the same cannot be said of the pro-choice movement. Mainstream feminist organizations aimed to work with, not against, the self-described pro-choice president—even as Clinton allowed the right wing to undermine the legal basis for women's right to choose. Clinton's 1992 campaign promise to pass a Freedom of Choice Act vanished soon after he took office. With a Democrat in the White House and a Democratic majority in Congress, the Freedom of Choice Act never even made it to the House floor for debate in 1993. That same year the Hyde Amendment—the federal ban on Medicaid abortion that is reapproved annually in the budget—sailed through the Democratic-controlled Congress. Many of the same Democrats who voted to renew Hyde were pro-choice candidates who had taken money from pro-choice organizations.[22]

The pro-choice movement could have—and should have—pursued a strategy that could galvanize the pro-choice majority into a fighting force to defend abortion rights. On April 9, 1989, at least 300,000 pro-choice activists demonstrated in Washington, D.C., to show their determination to fight for the right to legal abortion. In 1992, an even larger crowd—at least 500,000—turned out to defend the right to choose. The potential for building a mass movement tying abortion rights to women's rights was as clear then as it is now.

But already by the late-1980s, the leaders of the largest pro-choice organizations, such as the National Abortion Rights and Reproductive Rights Action League (now named NARAL Pro-Choice America) had made a conscious choice to shift its polemic on choice to one that would "play" on Capitol Hill—and with the "mushy middle" swing voters. NARAL issued a "talking points" memo to its affiliates in

1989, instructing staffers specifically not to use phrases such as "a woman's body is her own to control." Rather, the right to choose was to be cast as a right to "privacy."[23] Increasingly, pro-choice organizations emphasized that being pro-choice also meant being "pro-family"—giving up crucial ideological ground to the main slogan of the Christian Right.

No national pro-choice marches took place in Washington, D.C., between the election years of 1992 and 2004—even though the anti-abortion movement rallied by the thousands there each January 22, the anniversary of the *Roe v. Wade* decision. When Clinton broke his campaign promise to pass the Freedom of Choice Act, the pro-choice movement did not organize mass protests to hold him accountable. And when Clinton fulfilled his campaign promise to "end welfare as we know it" in 1996, signing Republican-sponsored legislation eliminating the federal welfare program, Aid to Families with Dependent Children (AFDC), pro-choice leaders did not lend activist support to the many thousands of poor women and children thrown off welfare.

Clinton voiced no disapproval as right-wing lawmakers passed state laws across the country mandating waiting periods, parental consent or notification, and a host of other restrictions on women's right to choose. Although Clinton formally opposed the Hyde Amendment, he did support the right of states to ban Medicaid abortion funding—as long as they included exceptions in cases of rape and incest. As Clinton said, "It's one thing to say that the taxpayers should not pay for a legal abortion that arises from a poor woman's own decision. That's one thing. Quite another to say the same rules apply to rape and incest."[24]

Even when Clinton vetoed Congress' initial attempts to ban the intact dilation and evacuation (intact D&E) abortion procedure—the first Congressional ban on so-called "partial birth abortion"—he appeased abortion opponents, saying he would be willing to sign a ban that made an exception to protect the woman's health. While waiting for Congress to act to ban intact D&E abortions, a number of states went ahead and passed "partial birth abortion" bans of their own.

Clinton's first term as president witnessed the most anti-choice voting record in Congress' history, yet Clinton's only attention to the abortion issue in his second term was to promote sexual abstinence among teens to lower the country's abortion rate. In 1997, Hillary Clinton urged the pro-choice movement to reject "extremism" and start forging unity with abortion foes on points of agreement, such as lowering the abortion rate in the United States.[25]

Yet mainstream pro-choice organizations continued to take their lead from the Clinton administration. Throughout Clinton's presidency, pro-choice "protests" were by and large limited to issuing press releases against the multitude of new restrictions on abortion, while "activism" revolved around campaigning for pro-choice Democrats. For example, NARAL embarked on a campaign in 1997 to help the Clinton administration in reducing the number of unplanned pregnancies by 30 percent. "People would like to see fewer abortions," echoed NARAL leader Kate Michelman at the league's annual luncheon celebrating the twenty-fourth anniversary of the right to legal abortion.[26]

Clinton's 1996 reelection campaign ads emphasized that he had signed a ban on gay marriage, the Defense of Marriage Act, and "required teen mothers on welfare to stay in school or lose benefits." Yet the pro-choice movement's support for Clinton's reelection never waned.[27]

By the end of Clinton's second term, women's right to choose was far more restricted than when he took office in 1993. Clinton's presidency shows why politicians cannot be relied upon to defend abortion rights—whatever their campaign rhetoric. Rather than a step forward for abortion rights, Clinton's presidency was a significant step backward.

George W. Bush targets abortion

Within days of taking office, Bush launched a frontal assault on abortion rights. Two days after his 2001 inauguration, Bush reinstituted a Reagan era global "gag" rule—overturned by Clinton—which denies U.S. family planning funds to any organization that mentions the option of abortion to pregnant patients during counseling. All international family planning agencies receiving U.S. funding are banned from even using their own money to provide abortion funding or counseling, effectively denying the right to choose to millions of poor women around the world faced with unplanned pregnancies. But no such restrictions on U.S. funds were placed on overseas sterilization programs in poor countries—which have left scores of women and men sterilized without their knowledge or consent over a period of decades.

Bush's attack on abortion rights is potentially much more far-reaching. Early on, he signaled his willingness to reverse the legal right to choose. On January 22, 2001, the twenty-eighth anniversary of *Roe v. Wade,* Bush told an NBC News reporter, "I've always said that *Roe v. Wade* was a judicial reach." Just days earlier, Bush remarked in an interview with Fox News that he would not rule out the possibility of having his new Justice Department argue for a change in the law.[28]

It is no accident that Bush launched an attack on abortion rights alongside his plan to deliver a massive tax cut to the rich, and subsequent attacks on affirmative action and gay marriage. By launching an assault on all things liberal, the Bush administration believed from the beginning that it could sideline the opposition, as Reagan had done two decades earlier. His election, like Reagan's, emboldened the Christian Right to aggressively pursue its "family values" agenda.

The attacks of September 11 gave Bush an excuse to launch an open-ended "war on terrorism" and advance the "Bush Doctrine" of "preemptive strikes" against its enemies—resulting in a quagmire of war and occupation in Afghanistan, followed by war and occupation in Iraq. At home, the Bush administration, while claiming the mantle of a "president in wartime," accused its critics of "aiding terrorists" as it pushed through a neoconservative program pandering to the Christian Right.

In 2002, the Bush administration withdrew U.S. ratification of the United Nations' "Convention on the Elimination of All Forms of Discrimination Against Women," that would require the world's governments to guarantee women the same legal rights and access to health care as men. That same year, Bush blocked $34 million in U.S. funding—previously approved by Congress—to the United Nations Population Fund (UNPF), an agency that does not offer abortion but provides maternity health services to poor women without access to hospitals.

The UNPF provides emergency birthing kits to Afghan women, who have the highest rate of maternal mortality in the world—the very women, in fact, that Bush claimed to be "liberating" during the war in Afghanistan.

In November 2003, George Bush made good on his pledge to sign a Congressional ban on the abortion procedure now widely known as partial birth abortion—the anti-choice movement's deceptive label, unknown in the world of medicine, yet adopted by the mass media. The procedure is extremely rare (fewer than .05 percent of all abortions) and is the most medically appropriate procedure for some women in the second or third trimesters. Banning this medically necessary procedure will endanger those women's lives or health—yet the ban passed through Congress without so much as a clause to protect the health of the pregnant woman. Although the fate of this abortion ban awaits a court decision on its constitutionality, Bush's signature on it scored a major public relations victory for the anti-abortion crusade.

Such a ban reinforces the false impression promoted by the anti-abortion crusade that women choose late-term abortions for "frivolous" reasons, when third trimester abortions are performed only under the most traumatic and heart-breaking circumstances—to save the life or health of a woman, or if the fetus is severely deformed.

Over the last twenty years, states across the U.S. have passed hundreds of laws curtailing women's right to choose—imposing mandatory twenty-four-hour waiting periods, requiring teenagers to notify or obtain the consent of their parents even in abusive families, and refusing state funding for poor women's abortions even if they have cancer or diabetes. In March 2004, the Senate passed the "Unborn Victims of Violence Act," making it a second crime to harm the fetus of a pregnant woman. And the right to legal abortion itself is in peril.

Will legal abortion be overturned?

In its July 3, 1989, ruling on *Webster v. Reproductive Health Services*, the United States Supreme Court came within one vote of overturning *Roe v. Wade*.[29] This example shows that legal abortion can be overturned. But the outcome is not pre-determined, nor is it dependent upon whether pro-choice politicians dominate Congress or occupy the White House.

Today, the Democratic Party is officially pro-choice and the Republicans are against the right to choose. But as recently as the mid-1970s, many prominent Republicans—including President Gerald Ford and then-Senator George H.W. Bush (the first President Bush)—were also pro-choice. In the 1960s, in fact, Bush Sr. had been an ardent promoter of birth control clinics for women. He became opposed to abortion only when he became Ronald Reagan's running mate in 1980.

Ruling-class opinion changes with the changing needs of the capitalist system. And the role of women within the system has changed a great deal over the last century.

The shifting needs of capitalism explain why abortion only became illegal in the mid-nineteenth century. Until that time, early abortions were widespread and legal. Abortions "before quickening" (fetal movement in about the fifth month of pregnancy) were socially acceptable for many centuries as a means of controlling fertility.

The introduction of anti-abortion legislation beginning in the middle of the nineteenth century—not to mention the Catholic Church's newfound opposition—was rooted in the needs of a rapidly industrializing economy. Between 1870 and 1929, the output of U.S. industry increased by fourteen times.[30] This created an enormous demand for new labor, which was filled in two main ways.

First, the U.S. government opened its doors to immigration. Before the outbreak of the First World War, foreign-born workers made up almost 60 percent of the industrial labor force in the United States.[31]

Second, working-class women and men were pressured to live in families in which women would be full-time homemakers and mothers, rather than full-time workers outside the home. In reality, most working-class women found some way to combine homemaking with earning money. Nevertheless, in 1900 only 5.6 percent of all married women were employed outside the home, according to census figures. In the United States, the birthrate was cut in half during the nineteenth century, but women continued to have a large number of children until the 1920s, when fertility rates dropped sharply.[32]

Ruling-class interests during this period clearly lay with promoting high birthrates. To this end, anti-abortion legislation spread to all fifty states. At the same time, textbooks and magazines were flooded with "expert" opinions expounding upon women's natural preference for full-time motherhood.

But as the twentieth century progressed, capitalism no longer needed women primarily in the home. By mid-century, higher American living standards meant lower infant mortality and fertility rates for individual women. Improvements in birth control methods—especially the introduction of the pill in the 1960s—allowed women to exercise more control in limiting pregnancy. Women thus became more desirable as workers to individual employers.

The trend since the Second World War has been for women workers to serve as a lower paid section of the labor force. Today, more than 70 percent of women of childbearing age are in the workforce. And the most dramatic increase has been in the number of working mothers: By 2002, 56.1 percent of mothers with children under the age of one were in the labor force.[33]

This is not, of course, to argue that capitalism no longer depends upon women to bear the primary responsibility for housework and child care within the family. As the Bureau of Labor Statistics explained, women have "increasingly added the role of worker to their more traditional family responsibilities."[34] The system needs women to be both homemakers and workers. Most working mothers actually have two jobs: one, a paid job, and the other, unpaid, in the home.

Divisions between the anti- and pro-choice factions of the ruling class over the issue of abortion reflect these contradictory roles that women fulfill. Family values ideology and anti-abortion ravings of right-wingers play an important role in whipping up support for the nuclear family. These ideas reinforce the notion that it is natural for women to want to take full responsibility for fulfilling all the needs of their families.

But women workers' control over pregnancy is necessary to maintain a stable workforce of lower-paid women workers. Hence, the support for legal abortion among such a wide swathe of capitalists.

These two wings of capitalists are not necessarily as far

apart as they seem. After all, many Republicans switched sides on the abortion debate since the 1970s, as have numerous Democrats. They usually explain their change of position on abortion to "personal journeys" leading to changes of "conscience." In reality, they have their fingers to the wind seeking a voting base.

And the politicians of *both* parties have shifted rightward since the 1970s. The shift rightward in the political climate that accompanied the rise of the Christian Right in the 1980s affected Democrats and Republicans alike. While politicians such as Bush and Lott act as spokesmen for the Christian Right, Democrats Bill Clinton and John Kerry also tout family values.

When Bill Clinton signed the 1996 Defense of Marriage Act and promoted teen abstinence while president, he was attempting to appease the Christian Right. When John Kerry made clear his opposition to gay marriage while on the 2004 presidential campaign trail, he was doing the same.

Republicans and Democrats alike represent corporate interests—and uphold the nuclear family as an institution that is central to capitalist society. Preserving the institution of the nuclear family, and most importantly women's unpaid labor within it, is of material benefit to the system.

The movement we need: Abortion without apology

How has the Christian Right been so successful at shifting the political climate? And how can we shift it back in the other direction? This is the crucial question facing pro-choice activists.

While a slim majority of Americans today continue to support the right to choose, current opinion polls show a majority favor further restrictions—and a majority also supports the so-called "partial birth" abortion ban.[35] These statistics demonstrate the success of the Christian Right's strategy of whittling away at the right to choose—but they are also a testament to the failure of the women's movement to successfully defend abortion rights.

For more than a decade, while the anti-abortion movement has been relentlessly pursuing an activist strategy to promote a variety of restrictions on abortion, it has faced little in the way of activist opposition from the pro-choice majority. Instead of mounting an unapologetic defense of women's right to control their own bodies, mainstream pro-choice organizations, like NARAL and Planned Parenthood, have increasingly spent the bulk of their time and money campaigning for pro-choice Democrats.

The bankruptcy of this strategy was demonstrated once again in November 2003, when sixty-three House Democrats and eleven Senate Democrats—including a number of self-described pro-choice Democrats—voted in favor of the misnamed partial birth abortion ban. And again in March 2004, forty-seven House Democrats joined forces with Republicans in voting for the Unborn Victims of Violence Act.

The inherent problem with entrusting pro-choice politicians to defend the right to choose has been obvious since Clinton's presidency. Yet, the pro-choice movement's main strategy has not swayed from its single-minded goal of electing Democrats into office. Thus, the 2004 March for Women's Lives, while massive in numbers, was entirely geared toward running Bush out of office in November—not building on the presence of one million pro-choice demonstrators to organize a grassroots movement to fight for abortion rights. A string of Democrats, such as Senator Hillary Rodham Clinton—who supported all of Bill Clinton's policies—made campaign speeches for John Kerry. Former Secretary of State Madeleine Albright—who oversaw the 1990s-era sanctions against Iraq that killed more than a million Iraqis—was offered a place of honor at the front of the march, despite her utter disregard for *Iraqi women's* lives.

This strategy sometimes works at winning votes on Election Day. But it is disastrous for social movements, whose goal is to change society, not to pander to the status quo as defined by the political mainstream. In adopting slogans based upon candidates' "electability," the pro-choice movement has ceded ideological ground to those forces aiming to curtail or overturn women's right to control their own bodies and reproductive lives.

After losing the 2004 presidential election, the Democrats signaled a further lurch to the right—toward abortion opponents. "We can all recognize that abortion in many ways represents a sad, even tragic, choice to many, many women," Senator Hillary Clinton said on January 24, 2005. She argued further that organized religion is the "primary" reason teenagers abstain from sex. She embraced the "opportunity for people of good faith to find common ground in this debate."[36]

The pro-choice movement must confront the fact that embracing a strategy that is mainly electoral has failed to turn the tide back in favor of abortion rights. Worse still, this strategy accepts the logic of politicians—that orienting to the political "center" is the key to success. In reality, this strategy has proven an abysmal failure.

An unapologetic defense of abortion rights, which links the right to choose with the fight for women's equality, is the only way to begin to shift the political climate. Women need the right to abortion in order to control their own bodies and reproductive lives. And no woman should ever be asked to justify why she chose to have an abortion, as if some reasons are morally acceptable while others are not. Finally, access to affordable abortion should be offered to every woman, as a part of basic health care.

Activism and solidarity are also needed to build the kind of movement that can turn the tide back in favor of abortion rights, whichever party is in the White House. This is the lesson from the women's liberation movement of the 1960s—which won the right to abortion in the first place. At the time abortion became legal, Richard Nixon—an anti-abortion right-winger much like George W. Bush—occupied the White House, and the Supreme Court was packed with conservative appointees. And the first state to make abortion legal was California in 1970—when none other than Ronald Reagan was governor.

President Nixon's rhetoric was indistinguishable from the Christian Right today. He argued in 1971,

> From personal and religious beliefs, I consider abortion an unacceptable form of population control. Further, unrestricted abortion policies, or abortion on demand, I cannot square with my personal belief in the sanctity of human life–including the life of the yet unborn....

To this statement, the New York Women's Strike Coalition responded, "We will grant Mr. Nixon the freedom to take care of his uterus if he will let us take care of ours."[37]

On August 26, 1970, the women's movement called a national day of action, Women's Strike for Equality, which brought over 50,000 women out to demonstrate for women's rights across the country. These demonstrations also called for free abortion on demand. Literally hundreds of local protests took place between 1969 and 1973 in favor of legal abortion.

But more important than the actual numbers drawn into the movement itself, the ideas of women's liberation found a much larger audience in the population at large. Effective social movements have a transforming impact on popular opinion. The effects of the women's movement were far-reaching in affecting the consciousness and expectations of millions of women workers and students. It brought the issues of equal pay, child care, and abortion rights into the national limelight. By 1976, a Harris survey reported that 65 percent of American women supported "efforts to strengthen and change women's status in society."[38] The persistence of the movement itself, along with the leftward shift of the general political climate generated by the antiwar, Black Power, and gay liberation movements pushed the political balance in favor of abortion.

Today, we need activism to build the kind of movement that can link the right to choose with full reproductive rights for all women—and can become a movement that will settle for nothing less than full equality.

Real people are living lives that are completely out of sync with the so-called family values of the Christian Right. We are in the majority, not the Christian Right. The vast majority of women today are in the workforce, while half of all marriages end in divorce. And the demand for gay marriage is a result of the fact that many same-sex couples are choosing to live together and raise families.

The pro-choice movement should be fighting against everything the Christian Right stands for. Such a movement—that defends the right to abortion without apology—will find millions of people on its side.

CHAPTER 3

What Ever Happened to Feminism?

BY ANY meaningful measure, women in the United States—and around the world—have not won equality with men. The fact that women's wages are on average about 75 percent of men's today—compared with a measly 59 percent in the late 1970s—is often cited as "proof" that women have made great strides. But a closer look shows that the closing wage gap is not due to higher wages for women, but rather to the fall in men's wages over the last thirty years. This is hardly a reason to celebrate for workers—of either sex.

In fact, in many respects, women have actually lost ground since the 1970s. One of the biggest victories of the women's movement was the legalization of abortion in 1973. Today, however, abortions are less accessible than thirty years ago. This fact was graphically illustrated in May 1998, when every single abortion clinic in the state of Wisconsin stopped performing abortions for two days after a bill was passed there that made it a crime punishable by mandatory life imprisonment for a doctor to perform the type of abortion procedure known as intact dilation and evacuation (intact D&E, which anti-abortion zealots have deceptively labeled "partial birth" abortion) *at any time after the moment of conception.*[1]

Although George W. Bush signed a federal ban on intact D&E abortion procedures, much of the damage was done before he took office. During Clinton's presidency, most states passed bans on intact D&E. In July 1998, the House of Representatives passed a law making it a crime for any adult to accompany a minor across state lines to have an abortion. Given these sorts of examples, there can be no question that Clinton's presence in the White House did little to stave off the attacks on abortion. Even though he had promised pro-choice voters in his 1992 presidential campaign that he would pass a Freedom of Choice Act to guarantee women's right to choose, he never mentioned it again after taking office.

Women's rights were set back in other arenas as well while Clinton was in office. To be sure, the Republican flap over Clinton's dalliance with Monica Lewinsky—an affair between two consenting adults—was an exercise in hypocrisy orchestrated by right-wingers. But the Lewinsky scandal was preceded by the Paula Jones sexual harassment lawsuit against Clinton. This case—and the Arkansas judge's dismissal of it—was an enormous setback for women's rights at the workplace.

The importance of the case has nothing to do with whether or not Paula Jones' claim that Clinton sexually harassed her is true. Her version of the story is that, back in the early 1990s, when he was governor of Arkansas and she was a low-level clerk working for the state, he tried to force himself on her sexually, then dropped his pants and exposed himself to her; when she got away from him, he grabbed her and warned that she had better be quiet about what happened between them.

The importance of the case has to do with the judge's complete dismissal of it. The judge argued that, even if Paula Jones was telling the truth, her case had no merit, that Clinton's behavior may have been "boorish and offensive," but these were just "brief and isolated episodes," which are acceptable between an employer and employee. In other words, it is perfectly legal for an employer to expose himself to a female underling, tell her to keep her mouth shut in a veiled threat, and attempt to solicit her through a third party (in Clinton's case, a state police officer who he sent as his messenger on more than one occasion)—all this is okay, as long as *eventually* he accepts rejection.[2]

One would have expected voices of outrage from feminists over the Paula Jones decision. But for the most part what came from the feminist camp was silence—so much silence that *Time* magazine's front cover asked in June 1998, "Is Feminism Dead?" The article argued that feminists are out of touch with the real issues of inequality facing women.

It describes an opinion poll of women across the United States showing that the top complaints for women were: 1) inequality in the workplace; 2) difficulties balancing work and family responsibilities; and 3) lack of quality child care.[3]

Feminists today not only tend to ignore these issues, but when they do break their silence, they often appear to be on the other side on issues that were crystal clear in the earlier days of the modern women's movement. Some of the very same feminists—most notably, Gloria Steinem, one of the founders of the 1960s women's movement—seem to have turned their backs on some of the main principles of the women's liberation movement. Slogans that defined the movement were turned on their heads in the 1990s. The slogan "yes means yes, no means no" raised mass consciousness about rape and sexual harassment in the 1970s, asserting that women should not be subjected to unwanted sexual advances. The idea that women alone deserve the right to control their own bodies, without interference from the church, the state, parents, or boyfriends was the underpinning of the pro-choice movement.

But these once sacred principles are fast disappearing, replaced by new slogans and new principles championed by feminists today.

The spokespeople for feminism in the late 1990s could easily have been mistaken for the anti-feminists they once denounced. There is no better example than the many well-known feminists whose comments filled editorial pages in 1998 denouncing Paula Jones. The National Organization for Women (NOW) actually took a formal poll of its chapters and amid great pomp and circumstance announced that it would NOT submit a brief supporting Paula Jones' legal appeal. Gloria Steinem wrote a *New York Times* editorial in which she defended Clinton, arguing that, although "Clinton may be a candidate for sex addiction therapy," feminists must continue to stand behind him because Clinton is "vital" to preserving reproductive freedom *and* because he eventually took no for an answer from Jones. Moreover, she pondered, shifting the blame to society's prudish attitudes, "Perhaps we have a responsibility to make it okay for politicians to tell the truth."[4]

Even Anita Hill—whose very name brings forth images of a courageous woman who was skewered in a televised 1991 Senate hearing after charging Supreme Court Justice Clarence Thomas with sexual harassment—joined the smear campaign against Paula Jones. She wrote an editorial in the *New York Times* that argued Clinton could not be guilty of sexually harassing Paula Jones because "there is little evidence that Ms. Jones suffered employment-related repercussions as a result of the incident."[5] One could venture to point out that there was also little evidence that Anita Hill suffered employment-related repercussions as a result of Clarence Thomas's suggestively pointing out pubic hairs on his Coca-Cola can—one of Anita Hill's complaints—yet feminists as a group correctly supported Anita Hill in 1991.

Susan Faludi, one of the most celebrated feminist writers of the 1990s, wrote the book *Backlash* in 1991, which told the truth about the conditions of everyday women's lives and the right-wing efforts to turn back the clock against women's rights. But even Susan Faludi sang a very different tune on the Paula Jones case. In an article that featured prominently in the liberal publication the *Nation*, Faludi ridiculed Jones: "I think we can safely conclude that Paula Jones will not expire from whatever a brief brush with Clinton might have entailed all those years ago; so far, she seems in the pink of health."[6]

Faludi then went on to argue that women must change *their* attitudes if they want to have power in the workplace, because

> one hallmark of having true power is not having to be reflex-
> ive in your responses. Because, along with the other powers
> comes the power to forgive men—to see one's grievance in
> proportion and not in the garish caricatures of Gothic ro-
> mance."[7]

It is true that Paula Jones had the support of every right-wing Clinton-hater, including the anti-abortion-rights zealot Randall Terry of Operation Rescue fame. Jones herself was, generally speaking, a conservative. But these factors have nothing to do with whether she was a victim of sexual harassment. Anita Hill herself was hardly a supporter of left-wing causes when feminists supported her claim of sexual harassment in 1991. Paula Jones' conservative base of support was the excuse used by feminists for abandoning her case, but hers was not an isolated incident. In reality there is a much broader and more significant shift taking place among feminists.

Leading feminists in the 1990s began campaigning to downplay virtually every aspect of women's oppression. Susan Faludi touches on this new theme in her comments in the *Nation*—if women want rights they have to learn how to stop seeing themselves as victims and begin taking responsibility for their actions.

This new approach to feminism was best summarized by feminist author Naomi Wolf, in her 1994 book *Fire with Fire*. In it, she coins the term "power feminism" as an alternative to what she calls "victim feminism"—"old habits left over from the revolutionary left of the 1960s—such as reflexive anticapitalism, an insider-outsider mentality, and an aversion to 'the system.'"[8]

Wolf admits that capitalism "does oppress the many for the few,"[9] but she argues that "enough money buys a woman out of a lot of sex oppression." That, in a nutshell, is Wolf's message. Women should embrace capitalism and get as much money and power for themselves as they can. She argues, bastardizing Marxism, "pending the 'revolution,' women are better off with the means of production in their own hands.... Women's businesses can be the power cells of the 21st century."[10]

But according to Wolf, women can only accomplish this goal if they stop seeing themselves as victims. After all, she writes, "If we stay hunkered down, defensive and angry, we waste our energies."[11] And, quoting then-First-Lady Hillary Clinton, she adds, "Who wants to walk around with clenched fists all the time?"[12] Thus she concludes, power feminism means "practicing tolerance rather than self righteousness."[13]

Wolf maintains that if women would stop focusing on all the things that are wrong with their lives and start thinking of themselves as powerful human beings, they could end oppression. All it takes, it seems, is change on a mass psychological level in order for women to embrace the many opportunities to raise themselves up as entrepreneurs and high-ranking politicians. As an example, she offers:

> An advertisement that shows the swearing in of a woman president can have as much or more power to advance women's historical progress as can the passage of the Equal Rights Amendment on the political level."[14]

Women are held back today, Wolf argues, not primarily because of discrimination within society, but by themselves. She says that women hold themselves back because of the "fear of having too much." Women are no longer hampered by economic or political obstacles in the way of equality, but quite simply by their own psychological negativity. "The question to ask," she writes, "is not whether society is ready to yield to women their rightful places, but whether women themselves are ready to take possession of them."[15] If only women would stop seeing themselves as victims, her logic goes, they would stop being victimized. If only women would embrace capitalism, they would stop being oppressed by it. If only women would stop being angry, they would be happy.

This individualistic approach to feminist change has been embraced by Gloria Steinem as well. She wrote a book in the early 1990s with a title that summarizes its content: *Revolution from Within: A Book of Self-Esteem.* The book ends with this guide to daily meditation, to help the reader achieve her life goals:

> There are many ways of meeting your future self. Imagining a figure ahead of you on life's path is one way. You might also think about a desired future event and imagine your future self within it. Or imagine a protecting future self who advises you in hard times, celebrates in good ones and is always there for you to ask: What would my guide say?... As your current self, say "I will become you." As your future self, say "I'll always be inside you."... Make a new section for this future self. You will be visiting each other often.[16]

This new, seemingly psychological approach to feminism—be it Naomi Wolf's mass psychic phenomena or Gloria Steinem's daily meditation with present and future selves—is actually based upon complete acceptance of even the most barbaric aspects of capitalist society, including war and class conflict. Naomi Wolf, for example, offers as a concrete example of power feminism American women combat soldiers during the 1991 Persian Gulf War. "[I]mages of women wielding real firepower shook loose the blinkers that keep women from imagining themselves as beings who can elicit not just love and desire, but respect and even fear," she gushes.[17] The 200,000 Iraqis, many of them women and children civilians, who were killed by the U.S. and its allies in the carpet bombing of Iraq during the 1991 Gulf War don't even merit a mention by Wolf.

Wolf embraces not only the pursuit of profits, but the class antagonism that goes with it. Although she does not dwell on the subject, she admits that for every woman who succeeds in business, there are many other women who cannot. After all, this is the nature of capitalism—someone actually has to produce profits, or there would be no managers. But class differences between women are not a cause for concern:

> There are going to be times when woman to woman aggression is a healthy, even energizing corollary of our having reached full participation in society.... Women are managing, criticizing and firing other women, and their employees sometimes, understandably, hate their guts.[18]

Moreover, she argues, power feminists should welcome any and all antagonisms that might be produced by the scapegoating and discrimination that takes place in class society:

> We are maturing into the understanding that women of different classes, races and sexualities have different, and often competing, agendas. Those conflicts should not be a source of guilt to us. They do not represent a breakdown of sisterhood. In the fullness of diversity, they represent its triumph.[19]

What is abundantly clear from the remarks quoted above is

that Naomi Wolf is concerned only with that minority of women who are climbing the corporate ladder—power feminists in business suits, who return home to a house that gets cleaned by a domestic servant and children whose needs are cared for by someone else, usually other women. Working-class women—who *do* have plenty of reason to complain about low wages or lack of adequate child care or decent health care—are mentioned only in passing. They are the women getting fired by or cleaning the homes of power feminists.

Power feminism allows women managers to convince themselves that they are bettering humanity simply by taking powerful positions in business or government—when the only women they are enriching are themselves. Naomi Wolf recalls that the first sizable check she wrote to a women's organization

> made me feel powerful in a way that felt right.... I began to tithe my income. Paradoxically, the more steadily I did this, the greater the sense of possession and entitlement I then felt...learning about money, trying to make money yield money, and even trying to negotiate for more. Money was not just a selfish, dirty indulgence that made me part of an oppressive system. It was an agent of change.... Not only was it permissible to learn to ask for more, always more, but it was a political act. It was imperative."[20]

Once the class vantage point of power feminism becomes clear, all its other aspects fall neatly into place. Power feminism speaks only for upper-middle-class women whose main concern is climbing the corporate ladder. In their own self-interest, these women seek to minimize aspects of gender that have in the past been used to deny women access to corporate promotions—notions that women who become mothers take time off for maternity leave, or otherwise take off too much work time to care for their children, or the idea that women might file lawsuits against sexist male colleagues. Women in the corporate world tend to play down these aspects of women's oppression that separate them from their male colleagues, precisely because they want to get ahead.

This framework—the idea that if women want rights they need to take responsibility, which Susan Faludi spelled out in regard to the Paula Jones case—is what guides the attitudes of leading feminists today on issues as diverse as sexual harassment, maternity leave, and abortion rights. And while Naomi Wolf can be credited with giving power feminism its name, it has actually been around ever since women began entering management and the professions in larger numbers. NOW, the largest feminist organization, was formed with this group of women in mind in the 1960s. NOW has never fought to win reforms such as maternity leave, which benefit working-class women exclusively—even though the United States is one of only a few countries in the world that does not offer paid maternity leave to its women workers.

Moreover, NOW formally took a stand *against* the right to maternity leave in 1986 in the case of a woman bank worker who was fired from her job after she took six weeks off—without pay—after having a baby. In the case *California Savings and Loan v. Guerra*, NOW filed a friend of the court brief agreeing with the bank that allowing a woman to take maternity leave discriminates against men with "similar disabilities." NOW took the side of the bank management over that of the woman worker.[21]

This framework also guides the approach of feminists such as Naomi Wolf on the issue of abortion rights. Wolf has espoused her views on the issue of choice numerous times, and each time she sounds as if she actually opposes the right to choose more than the time before. In *Fire with Fire* she wrote, "the other side of having reproductive rights is taking reproductive responsibility."[22] Furthermore, she argued, "some of the most thoughtful feminists are beginning to describe abortion as violence against women."[23] In a 1997 editorial in the *New York Times*, Wolf stated, "What if we called policies that sustain, tolerate and even guarantee the highest abortion rate of any industrialized nation what they should be called: crimes against women?"[24] In the editorial, she called for supporters of choice to join forces with those who are against abortion to "reject extremism" and to lower the "shamefully high rate of abortion" in the United States.

Naomi Wolf's words were echoed even by Kate Michelman, then-president of the National Abortion and Reproductive Rights Action League (since renamed NARAL Pro-Choice America). NARAL did not call on the pro-choice movement to demonstrate against the ban on so-called partial birth abortions. And Michelman vowed in 1997 that NARAL would join with abortion opponents to lower the abortion rate—partly through programs encouraging teenage girls to abstain from sex. As she put it, "People would like to see fewer abortions."[25]

Without pressure from feminists to defend the right to abortion, the Democratic Party steadily retreated on choice. Retreat finally turned to surrender after John Kerry's defeat in 2004. In January 2005, on the thirty-second anniversary of the *Roe v. Wade* decision, Senator Hillary Clinton called abortion a "sad, even tragic choice" that shouldn't "ever have to be exercised, or only in very rare circumstances."[26] Soon after, Howard Dean, chairman of the Democratic National Committee, argued, "I don't think we need to be the pro-abortion party. Nobody's pro-abortion."[27]

Far from criticizing Clinton and Dean, Michelman—who assumed the role of Democratic Party strategist after retiring as NARAL's president—quickly voiced her approval. In a letter to the *New York Times*, Michelman stated, "Senator Clinton deserves praise for reaching out to anti-choice Americans."[28]

Has feminism changed—or are feminists of today betraying modern feminism's founding principles? While it is true that the Gloria Steinem of today is quite different than the Gloria Steinem of 1970—the change in feminism has not been qualitative. Occasional lip service aside, mainstream feminism has never sought to represent any other class of women than the upper-middle class. Feminism has merely evolved to reflect the changing circumstances of this class of women. *The Feminine Mystique*, the book by Betty Friedan that opened the door to modern feminism in 1963, gave voice to the plight of suburban, college educated middle-class women who felt trapped in their suburban homes. These women were well-educated but had no opportunity to pursue careers because sexist attitudes kept the doors of the corporate world closed to them.

To be sure, the 1950s and 1960s—when women were told they should spend every waking moment devoting themselves to husband and family—were horribly oppressive. Friedan describes in her book, for example, a typical report from a marketing firm with its patronizing view of the average suburban housewife: she

> "finds in housework a medium of expression for femininity and individuality"...she still feels "lazy, neglectful, haunted by guilt feelings" because she doesn't have enough work to do. The advertiser must manipulate her need for "a feeling of creativeness" into the buying of his product.... "Creativeness is the modern woman's dialectical answer to the problem of her changed position in the household. Thesis: I'm a housewife. Antithesis: I hate drudgery. Synthesis: I'm creative!" This means essentially that even though the housewife may buy canned food...she doesn't let it go at that. She has a great need for "doctoring up" the can and thus prove her personal participation and her concern with giving satisfaction to her family.[29]

But one can have sympathy with the need for middle-class

housewives to rebel against this sort of sexist rubbish without forgetting how much better off they were than working-class women, who have never had the luxury of concerning themselves with career fulfillment. Unfortunately, Friedan does not. She acknowledges class differences between women, but makes clear from the beginning that the book limits its discussion to the problems of suburban housewives. In the chapter called "The problem that has no name," she writes, "It is not caused by lack of material advantages; it may not even be felt by women preoccupied with desperate problems of hunger, poverty or illness."[30] She makes no further comment on the plight of those women who *are* preoccupied by problems of poverty, hunger, or illness.

The entire purpose of the *Feminine Mystique* is to convince middle-class, educated suburban housewives to find fulfillment through a career in business or the professions.

Friedan praises women who had shown the courage to seek well-paying careers, writing sympathetically that these women "had problems of course, tough ones—juggling their pregnancies, finding nurses and housekeepers, having to give up good assignments when their husbands were transferred."[31] She doesn't even deem it worthy to comment on the lives of the nursemaids and the housekeepers these career women hire, who also work all day but then return home to face housework and child care responsibilities of their own.

The "power feminism" of Naomi Wolf is concerned with

this very same class of women—only this is the next generation, who have broken out of the suburban housewife trap and climbed into management. Feminism, now as then, speaks for this class of women—who are a minority—who can achieve relative equality within the confines of capitalism. These women do not need special reforms like maternity leave or child care because they have the wealth to hire others—usually other women—to carry out these tasks.

For this reason, mainstream feminism cannot speak to the needs, much less the aspirations, of the vast majority of women—who can't buy their way out of any aspect of their oppression, and who can't gain access to the kinds of opportunities for education and career that would allow them to earn vast sums of money. For working-class women, there are no individual solutions to being overworked and underpaid. And, Naomi Wolf's claims to the contrary, it matters little to most working-class women whether their manager is a man or a woman.

That is why socialists have traditionally argued that feminism, as a solution to women's oppression, offers nothing to working-class women. Capitalism places virtually the entire responsibility for raising children on the shoulders of individual working-class families—from providing medical care and transportation to food, clothing, and other necessities of life. Low-income families must struggle to make ends meet, or go without necessities. And within the working-class family, the responsibility for housework and childrearing falls overwhelmingly upon working-class women, whether or not they hold a job outside the home. Capitalism has continued to depend upon this subjugation of working-class women, even as it has extended the corporate ladder to middle- and upper-class women.

Society already has the resources to provide universal medical care and child care, not to mention assistance with the heavier aspects of housework and laundry. But capitalism is organized around the quest for profits, rather than the fulfillment of people's needs. The oppression suffered by the vast majority of women can only be eradicated by targeting the capitalist system that breeds it. Working-class women—and men, for that matter—have everything to gain from fighting for a socialist society. There is no blueprint for what a socialist society will look like. That will be determined by the workers who struggle for it and win it. But the principles of revolutionary socialism are long-standing—production for need and an end to all forms of oppression and exploitation. For women, this will offer the opportunity for genuine equality with men.

Feminists have traditionally accused socialists of subordinating the fight against women's oppression to the class struggle. Yet socialists have held to the principles of women's liberation that long ago fell by the wayside for mainstream feminists, precisely *because* socialists fight for the interests of the entire working class.

CHAPTER 4

Women and Islam

Hijab ban: Racist hypocrisy

ON MARCH 3, 2004, the French Senate passed a law banning female students from wearing the hijab, the head covering worn by many Muslim women and girls, in public schools starting in September 2004. French law now prohibits not just the hijab, but all "signs and dress that ostensibly denote the religious belonging of students." It also bans beards and bandanas that denote Islamic affiliation, the Jewish yarmulka, or skullcap, and "conspicuous" Christian crosses. Nevertheless, few in France, where the press dubbed the ban "the law against the veil," believe the target is anything but the hijab.[1]

The French ban inspired lawmakers in Belgium and Germany to consider following suit. On April 1, 2004, the conservative state of Baden-Wurttemberg in Germany banned

Muslim public school teachers from wearing headscarves. The anti-hijab trend even extended to the United States, where a sixth-grade student in the Muskogee, Oklahoma public school district was suspended twice for wearing her hijab in 2003.[2]

France's move to ban the hijab generated heated controversy—dividing leftists, antiracists, feminists, and even some Muslims. A founder of the French antiracist organization SOS-Racisme resigned after it came out in support of the ban. Respected feminist Fadela Amara, president of Ni Putes Ni Soumises (Neither Whores Nor Downtrodden), an advocate group for North African women, supports the law. Some feminists oppose the law on the grounds that it will strengthen Islamic fundamentalism. In December 2003, Muhammad Sayyid Tantawi, grand sheikh of al-Azhar University in Cairo, publicly declared that Muslims living in non-Muslim countries are obliged to obey that country's laws, including a ban on wearing the hijab. But other high-ranking Islamic clerics strongly disputed this assertion, and argued that banning the hijab is a direct attack on Islam.[3]

Generally speaking, however, French progressives and feminists who support the law view it as a step forward for Muslim women's rights. On December 5, 2003, for example, sixty prominent French women, including actors Isabelle Adjani and Emmanuelle Béart, published a petition calling for an outright ban on the hijab, as a "visible symbol of the submission of women."[4]

But whatever the rationale among progressives for supporting the hijab ban, it cannot be judged apart from its role in the rising tide of racism against Muslim populations throughout Europe, and indeed, around the world. In this campaign, as *Middle East Report* editorial committee member Paul Silverstein argues, "Law-and-order right-wingers, including [French Interior Minister Nicolas] Sarkozy, view the law as an important weapon in their ongoing 'war on terror.'"[5]

French President Jacques Chirac's stated motivation for the ban is draped in references to the French Republican secular tradition. "Secularism is not negotiable," he proclaimed when proposing the ban in December 2003. And the Stasi Report, the government commission study on which Chirac based the new ban, defined the public school as a privileged "closed universe," which emphasizes values of male-female equality and mutual respect. The Stasi Report recommended a total of twenty-six measures, some intended to promote cultural diversity—such as adding the Jewish Yom Kippur and Islamic Eid al-Adha in addition to Christian public holidays, and teaching Berber and Kurdish languages to address these ethnic minorities. But only the ban on "ostensibly" religious dress was incorporated into French law.[6]

There is something profoundly hypocritical in banning Islamic religious symbols in the name of secularism and gen-

der equality while the French government continues to sub-
sidize private education for the globally influential—and reactionary—Catholic Church, as well as Jewish religious
institutions. Beneath French officials' talk of *laïcité* (separation of church and state), the status quo in French society is
Christianity. Prime Minister Jean-Pierre Raffarin even described France as "the old land of Christianity" during the
debate. The justice minister of one German state justified
banning the hijab by stating that German children "have to
learn the roots of Christian religion and European culture."[7]

It is just a short leap from the (stated and unstated) assumption of Christian religious and European cultural superiority to outright hostility to Islam. One German state
designated the hijab "a symbol of fundamentalism and extremism." Former French Prime Minister Alain Juppé argued, "It's not paranoid to say we're faced with a rise of
political and religious fanaticism." Jacques Peyrat, the mayor
of Nice—a far-right stronghold—argued in a speech,
"Mosques cannot be conceived of as existing within a secular Republic."[8]

Chirac's hostility toward Muslims, France's largest minority, was apparent when he argued on December 6, 2003,
"Wearing a veil, whether we want it or not, is a sort of aggression that is difficult for us to accept." Bernard Stasi,
head of Chirac's commission, was even more forthright in
defending the ban: "We must be lucid—there are in France

some behaviors which cannot be tolerated. There are without any doubt forces in France which are seeking to destabilize the republic, and it is time for the republic to act."[9]

Chirac and Stasi were chasing after the voters of France's second-largest political party, the far-right National Front of Jean-Marie Le Pen, who forced the center-right Chirac into a run off in the last presidential election. Le Pen argues that France's five million Arab immigrants bring crime to the streets, and they should "assimilate" into French society or be driven out. In 2002, 27.7 percent of voters from the Provence-Côte d'Azur-Alpes region—France's third-wealthiest, and a voting base for the National Front—backed Le Pen's "national preference" measures, including the enforced repatriation of immigrants.[10]

As Pierre Tévanian argued in *Le Monde diplomatique,*

Young Muslim women are being used as scapegoats, a focus of attention to distract France from rampant social inequality and deprivation, to take minds off deregulation, declining job security, encroachments on civil liberty, racial discrimination and gender inequality.[11]

In an equally racist manner, the French government also marketed the hijab ban as a strike against anti-Semitism—despite the fact that hate crimes against French Jews have historically been inflicted by forces of the far right. During the hijab debate, Education Minister Luc Ferry argued that the Middle East conflict "has entered our schools" and that France is facing an anti-Semitism "which is no longer of the extreme right, but of Islamic origin." In November 2003—just weeks before proposing the hijab ban—Chirac announced a new government commission to fight anti-Semitism, targeting the residents of North African neighborhoods for education against anti-Semitism.[12]

In reality, Muslims have been the primary targets of hate crimes in France (and throughout Europe) since the 1960s. Yet France's ministry of the interior does not even include a category for attacks directed against Muslims or North Africans, as it does with anti-Semitic attacks. Norman Madarasz summarized the targeted communities as follows:

> In England, with Pakistanis, in Germany, with the Turkish, and in France, Italy, Spain and Portugal, with immigrants from the al-Maghreb North African region: Moroccans, Algerians, Tunisians, Berbers, Cabyls, as well as Palestinians and sub-Saharan Muslims, especially from Mali.[13]

France's National Consultative Commission on Human Rights (CNCDH) documented hate crimes committed against Muslims in 2002—but noted that these examples "fall well under the real number" of racist attacks committed against Muslims. Below is a list of examples from the CNCDH report, published in *Le Monde* on November 24, 2003:

> While awaiting the 2003 statistics, the study lists several examples of serious violence committed in 2002: Molotov cocktails thrown at the mosques of Mericourt (in the Pas-de-Calais region) and Chalons (in the Marne region), on April 25 and 27, and on March 24 against the Ecaudin mosque (in the Rhône region); a letter bomb was sent to an

association seated at the Perpignan mosque (in the Pyrénées-Orientales), on April 9; an Islamic religious sculpture was profaned in Lyon, on April 24; attempted torching of a place of worship in Rillieux-la-Pape (Rhône), on December 27; anonymous tracts distributed during the presidential campaign [held in April 2002 which had set far-right racist candidate Jean-Marie Le Pen against the incumbent Chirac]. As for 2003, three facts can be pointed to: profaned tombs in the Haut-Rhin region in July, torching of a place of worship at Nancy, and profanation of an Islamic square in the Meuse region in March.[14]

In this context, France's ban on Islamic headscarves can only further inflame anti-Muslim racism. No law reeking of such racist hypocrisy is intended to advance the cause of women's equality.

Imperialism does not "liberate" women

Wittingly or not, feminists who support measures such as the hijab ban are supporting campaigns designed to exploit the Western symbol of Islamic women's oppression—the veil—to claim Western imperialism's cultural superiority, and bolster its domestic and global aims, all under the guise of fighting "Islamic terrorism."

Feminist support for Chirac's hijab ban in France has a more exaggerated, and therefore more transparent, parallel in the U.S. during the 2001 Afghan war. The Bush administration gained the support of mainstream U.S. feminists for the war on Afghanistan, who echoed his arguments that the war would "free" Afghan women from the tyranny of Taliban rule.

First Lady Laura Bush declared, "The fight against terrorism is also a fight for the rights and dignity of women." Feminist Majority president Eleanor Smeal embraced this claim, adding to the general post–September 11 hysteria by putting forward her own version of the "domino theory":

> We argued that the Talibanization of society would not stop in Afghanistan. We could see it moving into Pakistan, into Algiers and all through the Middle East to Turkey. We argued that it would lead to regional instability, and that this had much larger world ramifications than just what is happening to women there…. The link between the liberation of Afghan women and girls from the terrorist Taliban militia and preservation of democracy and freedom in America and worldwide has never been clearer.[15]

The Feminist Majority even circulated a petition thanking the Bush administration for its commitment to restoring the rights of women in Afghanistan. And feminists applauded Secretary of State Colin Powell when he proclaimed in November 2001, "The rights of women in Afghanistan will not be negotiable," as television cameras zoomed in to show smiling Afghan women lifting their veils.[16]

More than three years after the war, U.S. media outlets have not returned to report on the fate of women in post-Taliban Afghanistan. If they did, they would find that the majority of Afghan women, even in Kabul, continue to wear the burqa—head-to-toe Islamic covering. As Mariam Rawi of the Revolutionary Association of Women of Afghanistan (RAWA) argues, "the U.S. has replaced one misogynist fundamentalist regime with another."[17]

The Taliban's Department of Vice and Virtue has been resurrected under the name of the Ministry of Religious Affairs. Warlords responsible for a reign of terror between 1992 and 1996, including the mass rape and murder of women, remain in power throughout the countryside, enriching themselves through opium production. President Hamid Karzai appointed fundamentalist Fazl Hadi Shinwari as the chief justice of the Supreme Court. "Shinwari has packed the nine-member Supreme Court with 137 sympathetic mullahs and called for Taliban-style punishments to implement Shari'a law."[18]

After visiting Afghanistan, filmmaker Meena Nanji reported,

> The litany of laws passed this year governing women's conduct reads like a page out of the Taliban handbook. They include the banning of co-education classes, restrictions on women's ability to travel, the banning of women singing in public. The biggest blow yet to women's rights was dealt in November, when a 1970's law prohibiting married women from attending high school classes was upheld. This is a major step backwards for women and girls, as many underage girls are forced into marriage and now have no hope of improving their lives.[19]

This outcome should have been easy to predict. But in 2001, U.S. feminists never challenged the ridiculous notion that a right-wing Republican like Bush was taking a genuine interest in advancing women's rights. His presidency already had a track record. Two days after his inauguration in January 2001, Bush reinstated a Reagan-era global "gag" rule, denying U.S. funding to any international family planning organization that mentions the option of abortion to pregnant patients during counseling, effectively denying the right to choose to millions of poor women around the world faced with unplanned pregnancies. According to the World Health Organization, 78,000 women around the world die from unsafe abortions every year.[20]

Nevertheless, feminist endorsement for the war on Afghanistan helped the Bush administration to promote the fiction that the war aimed to "liberate" Afghan women. This illusion helped Bush gain support among a wide swathe of liberals and even antiwar activists in the United States—for the war that launched the "war without end" and led directly to the invasion and occupation of Iraq.

Furthermore, feminists such as Smeal, a regular guest on television news programs throughout the war, helped ratchet up anti-Muslim racism on the war's other front: the war at home. While the USA PATRIOT Act sailed through Congress after September 11, thousands of Muslims were rounded up and "detained indefinitely" without charges or the right to legal representation in the name of "fighting terrorism." In a typical rant, Smeal stated, "We have become the bad guys; they are blaming all of their economic ruin on the West. They think we don't like Muslims, so instead, they become more fundamentalist: 'We'll show you, we'll be more Muslim.'"[21]

European "cultural superiority" as justification for colonialism

France's ban on the hijab is not a new phenomenon, resulting from circumstances peculiar to "modern" society. The French government's current campaign against the hijab as a means to denigrate Islamic culture has its origins in colonial history. Imperialists and their apologists have claimed European cultural superiority as a justification for dominating Muslim societies since colonialism began. The reference points of Egypt's British colonizers a century ago, for example, bear a striking resemblance to those of U.S. and European imperialists today.

During the British occupation of Egypt, British Consul General Lord Cromer declared that Egyptians should "be persuaded or forced into imbibing the true spirit of Western civilization." Cromer targeted, "first and foremost," Islam's "degradation of women," symbolized by the veil, as "the fatal obstacle" to Egyptians' "attainment of that elevation of thought and character which should accompany the introduction of Western civilization."[22]

Cromer needed look no further than the corseted and repressed women of Victorian England for examples of the "degradation of women." Yet, as Egyptian feminist Leila Ahmed notes,

> This champion of the unveiling of women was, in England, the founding member and sometime president of the Men's League for Opposing Women's Suffrage. Feminism on the home front and feminism directed against white men was to

be resisted and suppressed; but taken abroad and directed against the culture of colonized peoples, it could be promoted in ways that admirably served the project of the dominance of the white man.[23]

Neither could Cromer's colonial policies in Egypt, which were aimed at developing the country's economy no further than as a supplier of raw materials for factories based in England, be described as advancing women's rights. Because he believed that government-subsidized education could foster nationalism, Cromer instituted school tuition fees, even though education was previously provided at government expense. The result: In 1881, the year before the British occupation began, 70 percent of Egyptian students received government assistance for tuition and other expenses. Ten years later, 73 percent of students received nothing. This severely curtailed educational opportunities for girls as well as boys.[24]

British occupation denied women opportunities for education on another front. Before British rule, Egyptian women had been offered equal medical training with men at the School for Hakimas. But the British limited women's training to midwifery. Once again, Cromer claimed cultural superiority: "I am aware that in exceptional cases women like to be treated by female doctors, but I conceive that throughout the civilized world, attendance by medical men is still the rule."[25]

Nevertheless, then—as now—imperialists were able to gain endorsements for their aims, under the guise of advancing women's rights. Ahmed argues:

> Whether in the hands of patriarchal men or feminists, the ideas of Western feminism functioned to morally justify the attack on native societies and to support the notion of the comprehensive superiority of Europe. Evidently, then, whatever the disagreements of feminism with white male domination within Western societies, outside their borders feminism turned from being the critic of the system of white male dominance to being its docile servant.[26]

Hostility to Islamic culture also found supporters inside the colonized countries, primarily among the rising upper- and upper-middle classes who benefited economically during colonialism. In 1899, *The Liberation of Women* appeared in Egypt, calling for banning the veil. Its author, Qassim Amin, a French-educated lawyer, was far less in favor of women's rights than the book's title suggests. Amin made clear he was "not among those who demand equality in education," instead recommending only primary education as necessary for women to fulfill their duties as wives and mothers. He based arguments on the need for assimilation with European culture, and described Egyptians as "lazy and always fleeing work."[27]

This phenomenon was by no means restricted to Egypt under colonial rule. During the twentieth century, other countries in the Muslim world imposed "Europeanization" on their own populations—banning aspects of Islamic culture and dress. In 1925, Kamal Ataturk, ruler of post–Ottoman Turkey, imposed the Hat Law, banning the traditional fez cap for men, under the penalty of death. In 1928, Reza Khan, Iran's shah, passed a law mandating European attire for men after seizing power. In 1936, he banned the hijab for Iranian women.[28]

Islam and resistance to imperialism

But if much of the upper class benefited from imperialism and aimed to emulate European culture, less prosperous sections of society rebelled—by defending Islam. The result was a strengthening of Islam as an expression of cultural identity, in opposition to the colonizers. Muslim organizations embraced and defended Islamic religious customs as a counterweight to imperialism. The Muslim Brotherhood, founded in Egypt in 1928, sought a return to a purified form of Islam—and a rejection of British domination. Its early members expressed that they were "weary of this life of humiliation and domination…. We see that the Arabs and Muslims have no status…and no dignity…. They are no more than mere hirelings belonging to foreigners."[29]

The growth of Islam, however, was just one form of resistance to colonialism and imperialism. By mid-century, the impact of Islamic movements was supplanted by the growing influence of Pan-Arabism, as secular nationalist—including communist—parties grew in size, and Pan-Arab leaders asserted and finally won independence, breaking the hold of colonialism. Pan-Arabism grew throughout the region after Abdel Nasser seized power in Egypt in 1952. To consolidate his own power, however, Nasser dissolved and banned all political parties in Egypt in 1953, brutally suppressing the Muslim Brotherhood.[30]

During the Cold War, the Soviet Union provided funding and support to a variety of anti-colonial movements and nationalist regimes around the world, including Nasser's. This support did not reflect a genuine political commitment to national self-determination, but rather resulted from the Cold War rivalry between the United States and the USSR—an imperialist competition to dominate whole regions of the world. Russia's hypocrisy became most obvious after its 1979 invasion and decade-long occupation of Afghanistan.

But the resurgence of Islam in recent decades also coincided with the relative decline in the strength and influence of Pan-Arab nationalism. Pan-Arabism declined for a number of reasons—among them, its failure to confront either class inequality within Arab societies or to pose a fundamental challenge to imperialism itself. During the 1970s—decades after winning independence—entrenched and corrupted local ruling classes, from Pahlavi's Iran to Sadat's Egypt, amassed personal fortunes by continuing to collaborate with imperialist powers—while continuing to emulate European cultural norms.

It is worth noting that the 1979 Iranian Revolution that overthrew the Pahlavi regime was preceded by a mass strike wave that raised a broad range of working-class and anti-im-

perialist demands—women's rights among them. A pro-
longed strike by oil workers in October 1978, for example,
listed as one of its eleven demands "an end to discrimination
against women staff employees and workers."[31] The subsequent "Islamic Revolution" involved the consolidation of Aya-
tollah Khomeini's repressive regime—and the dismantling of
Iranian workers' organizations coupled with the imposition of
reactionary religious law from above. The Iranian Revolution
was, therefore, far from a fanatical religious uprising.[32]

The fall of Stalinist rule in the USSR and Eastern Europe
at the beginning of the 1990s dealt an enormous blow to nationalist movements allied with the Soviet Union, and dis-
credited Stalinism. The fall of the Soviet Union put an end to
the Cold War—but the collapse of the USSR allowed the subsequent strengthening of U.S. imperialism, beginning with
the 1991 Gulf War. The current Bush administration's inva-
sions of Afghanistan and Iraq, not to mention the Bush Doctrine's assertion of "preemptive war" were not a break from,
but an acceleration of, a process that was well under way in
the early 1990s, years before September 11.[33]

Political forms of Islam can gain in strength and influence—as an expression of opposition to imperialism—in the
absence of a strong secular alternative. The decline of Pan-
Arabism, coupled with a strengthening of U.S. imperialism in
the 1990s, produced a widening identification with Islam as an
ideological counterweight to U.S. imperialism throughout the

Arab and Muslim world, and has grown further since the U.S. launched the "war on terrorism" following September 11.

Moreover, the United States and its staunchest Middle East ally, Israel, played a key role in building up the very "Islamic extremists" that their war on terrorism targets today. In the 1980s, Israel provided funding that helped to launch the Islamic-based Palestinian opposition movement, Hamas, in the hope of weakening the extensive influence of the secular-nationalist Palestine Liberation Organization (PLO) "One can be pretty sure that this strategy received strong encouragement from Washington, which has also seen the advantage of financing and supporting the most vicious and narrow-minded Islamic terrorists on account of their antinationalist and antisocialist credentials," wrote *New York Press* columnist George Szamuely.[34]

The United States provided $3 million for the build up of an Islamic fighting force, known as the Mujahideen, to oust the Soviet Union from Afghanistan in the 1980s. As journalist Ken Silverstein noted,

> few within the government had any illusions about the forces that the United States was backing. The Mujahideen fighters espoused a radical brand of Islam—some commanders were known to have thrown acid in the faces of women who refused to wear the veil—and committed horrific human rights violations in their war against the Red Army.[35]

As BBC foreign correspondent Matt Frei summarized,

The US and its allies plied this country with Stinger missiles and cash to fuel the Mujahideen's opposition against Soviet occupation. They encouraged the growth of Islamic fundamentalism to frighten Moscow and of drugs to get Soviet soldiers hooked. The CIA even helped "Arab Afghans" like Osama bin Laden, now "America's most wanted," to fight here.[36]

In the context of imperialism—and the racism that justifies imperialist domination—it is wrong to view the hijab, or other aspects of Islamic culture, only as symbols of women's oppression. Today, the hijab is worn voluntarily by millions of Muslim women around the world as a symbol of cultural pride, often in overt opposition to Western imperialism. After Chirac announced the ban on headscarves, tens of thousands of women wearing the hijab marched in protest across France, chanting slogans such as, "Not our fathers nor our husbands, we chose the headscarf." In London, thousands of young women wearing hijabs also marched, chanting against "racist laws." Their voices should not be ignored.[37]

Veiled or unveiled, women's oppression is universal

There is no contradiction between supporting Muslim women protesting the ban on headscarves in France and championing Afghan women in their fight against laws mandating the burqa. Women should have the right to dress as they choose wherever they live, without government interference. This should be a basic human right.

Moreover, feminists who allowed the Bush administration

to equate the lifting of the Islamic veil with liberation, and those who now argue that the France's hijab ban is a step toward women's equality, perform a disservice to the fight for genuine women's liberation, East and West. Journalist Natasha Walter recently expressed the common view among Western feminists: "Many women in the west find the headscarf deeply problematic. One of the reasons we find it so hateful is because the whole trajectory of feminism in the west has been tied up with the freedom to uncover ourselves."[38]

But the "freedom to uncover" can bring women no closer to genuine equality in a sexist society. In societies the world over, "uncovering" merely leads to greater sexual objectification. In the United States, eating disorders have reached epidemic proportions among young women, cosmetic surgery is one of the fastest-growing branches of modern medicine, and Hooters is a national restaurant chain. Jiggle movies like *Charlie's Angels* and *Tomb Raider* offer some of the best opportunities for career advancement for female actresses in Hollywood. And cartoon shows such as *Stripperella*—starring Erotica Jones, "a stripper by night and a superhero by later night"—target an ever-younger audience. Soon to join the primetime lineup is *Hef's Superbunnies*, a cartoon about Playboy Playmates who fight evil.[39]

Turkish society illustrates why "secularism" and "Westernization" do not automatically lead to women's liberation. Although Turkey's population is overwhelmingly Muslim, its government bans the hijab for women in educational institutions and government offices. But Turkey has imported Western sexist culture as well, including an endless barrage of demeaning sexist imagery. As political economist Behzad Yaghmaian described on a recent visit to Turkey, "Pictures of half-naked women were exhibited on billboards and in daily newspapers."

Yaghmaian described a woman student from Istanbul University, who said, "Hijab sends an important message that a person does not have to see my body to have a conversation with me."[40] This sentiment is valid and should not be dismissed by feminists. As a young Egyptian woman told reporters some years ago, she prefers the hijab because, "Many men treat women as objects, look at their beauty; the Islamic dress allows a woman to be looked upon as a human being and not an object."[41]

Nor is there truth to the common claim that Islam is more reactionary, more violent, or more oppressive to women than Christianity. Indeed, this claim is absurd, considering the 200-year history of the Christian Crusades wreaking death and destruction against Muslims and Jews. Pope Urban II launched the first crusade in a speech in 1095, calling on Christians to wage a "holy war" against Islamic "infidels."[42]

In more recent history, burning of hundreds of "witches" at the stake was practiced among the most self-righteous Christians in Europe, and in North America, as recently as

four centuries ago. And in current history, Christian fundamentalists have used the excuse of September 11 to incite ha-
tred and violence against Muslims. Shortly after September
11, evangelist Franklin Graham, now in charge of his father's
organization, the Billy Graham Evangelistic Association, declared: "The God of Islam is not the same God. He's not the
son of God of the Christian or Judeo-Christian faith. It's a different God, and I believe it is a very evil and wicked religion."
George W. Bush himself frequently invokes his Christian
"Almighty" as justification for the occupation of Iraq.[43]

It is impossible to generalize about the beliefs of Islam
any more than about the beliefs of Christianity or Judaism,
since there are as many different interpretations of the Koran
as there are competing interpretations of Biblical scripture.

Religion, class society, and women's oppression

It is possible, however, to document that in neither form
nor substance is women's oppression unique to Islam. As
Ahmed notes in her carefully-researched book, *Women and
Gender in Islam*, "[A] fierce misogyny was a distinct ingredi-
ent of Mediterranean and eventually Christian thought in the
centuries immediately preceding the rise of Islam," In addition, "The veil was apparently in use in Sasanian society, and
segregation of the sexes and use of the veil were heavily in
evidence in the Christian Middle East and Mediterranean regions at the time of the rise of Islam" in the seventh century

A.D.[44] Egyptian feminist Nawal el Saadawi has argued, "the most restrictive elements towards women can be found first in Judaism in the Old Testament, then in Christianity, and then in the Quran." Furthermore, el Saadawi argued, the "veiling of women isn't a specifically Islamic practice but an ancient cultural heritage with analogies in sister religions."[45]

Religions did not create oppressive human relationships in class society, but have functioned historically to enforce ideology that strengthens already existing inequalities within the social order.

Beliefs in supernatural forces, including male and female gods, preceded the rise of religion—as an attempt to comprehend forces of nature and their relation to human society. But organized religion could only have risen with the existence of settled communities, just as religious scriptures required the technology of writing. Organized religion rose hand in hand with the rise of class society, and its role evolved in tandem with the development of exploitation as the dominant relation of production.

Karl Marx and Frederick Engels argued that the shift away from the communal life of earlier hunter-gatherer societies and toward settled agriculture gave way to the rise of class society. Technological developments such as the plow and the domestication of cattle sharply increased the productivity of agriculture—for those owning land, plows, and cattle. For the first time in human history, it was possible for some people to accumulate wealth, creating a division between rich and poor.

It is important to understand that these changes did not take place overnight, or in identical succession across all societies. Nevertheless, large swathes of human society were transformed in similar ways over a period of thousands of years, with the rise of the first class societies some 6,000 years ago (first in Mesopotamia, followed a few hundred years later by Egypt, Iran, the Indus Valley, and China).[46]

Nor did the rise of class society take place without struggle and extreme brutality. Slavery was common, and the peasantry, robbed of their land and livelihood was reduced to destitution. Early Christianity—before it acquired a bureaucracy of its own—provided a voice for the downtrodden against the appalling division between rich and poor in the Roman Empire. The Christian religion developed during the decline of the Roman Empire, encompassing today's Italy and Spain, part of France, part of Turkey, Palestine, and other territories. The Polish revolutionary Rosa Luxemburg, in a 1905 pamphlet, "Socialism and the Churches," documented the outrage at class injustice shared by many early Christians, including Jesus Christ. Saint Basil, writing in the fourth century A.D., argued:

> Wretches, how will you justify yourselves before the Heavenly Judge? You say to me, "What is our fault, when we keep what belongs to us?" I ask you, "How did you get that which you called your property? How do the possessors become rich, if not by taking possession of things that belong to all?

> If everyone took only what he strictly needed, leaving the
> rest to others, there would be neither rich nor poor."[47]

But as the Church itself developed as an institution, be-
coming incorporated as the state religion of the Roman Empire in the fourth century, its interests became intertwined
with those of the nobility. From the sixth century on, the
Church began collecting taxes in its own right. "Thus,"
wrote Luxemburg,

> the poor people not only lost the help and support of the
> Church, but they saw the priests ally themselves with their
> other exploiters: princes, nobles, moneylenders. In the Mid-
> dle Ages, while the working people sank into poverty
> through serfdom, the Church grew richer and richer.[48]

Class society drastically lowered the status of women. For
property owners, agricultural production increased the demand for labor—the greater the number of field workers, the
higher the surplus. Thus, unlike hunter-gatherer societies,
which sought to limit the number of offspring, agricultural societies sought to maximize women's reproductive potential, so
the family would have more children to help out in the fields.

In communal hunter-gatherer societies, women had been
able to play a key role in production and public life, but agricultural production shifted away from the household. The
family no longer served anything but a reproductive function.
Women became trapped within their individual families, as
the reproducers of society—cut off from production for the
first time. Therefore, at the same time that men were playing

an increasingly exclusive role in production, women were required to play a much more central role in reproduction.

These changes brought about by class society were wholly degrading to women. As Engels noted in the *Origin of the Family, Private Property and the State*, the original meaning of "family" (familia) "was invented by the Romans to denote a new social organism whose head ruled over wife and children and a number of slaves, and was invested under Roman paternal power with rights of life and death over them all."

Engels continued:

> The man took command in the home also; the woman was degraded and reduced to servitude; she became the slave of his lust and a mere instrument for the production of children.... In order to make certain of the wife's fidelity and therefore the paternity of his children, she is delivered over unconditionally into the power of the husband; if he kills her, he is only exercising his rights.[49]

Engels did not exaggerate the degree of misogyny that accompanied this process. Assyrian (pre-Islamic) law in Mesopotamia allowed men to "pull out the hair of his wife, mutilate (or) twist her ears" in punishment. The Biblical writings of Augustine conclude of womankind, "I fail to see what use woman can be to man...if one excludes the function of bearing children."[50] By the Middle Ages, the Catholic Church codified into canon law the right of husbands to beat their wives.

Many of these changes in custom took place first among the property-owning families. But eventually, the family became the unit of reproduction in society as a whole. The veil, for example, was initially proscribed only for upper-class women (in Assyria, slaves were forbidden to veil[51]), functioning as a class delineator among women, but spread later as a common form of dress for all women.

As Ahmed describes, Islam, which did not emerge until these societal changes were well under way, inherited some religious customs from neighboring—and conquered—societies. Like Judaism and Christianity before it, Islam offered a divine sanction to women's extreme oppression in the new social order, as Ahmed describes:

> Islam placed relations between the sexes on a new footing. Implicit in this new order was the male right to control women and to interdict their interactions with other men. Thus the ground was prepared for the closures that would follow: women's exclusion from social activities in which they might have contact with men other than those with rights to their sexuality; their physical seclusion, soon to become the norm; and the institution of internal mechanisms for control, such as instilling the notion of submission as a woman's duty. The ground was thus prepared, in other words, for the passing of a society in which women were active participants in the affairs of their community and for women's place in Arabian society to become circumscribed in the way that it already was for their sisters in the rest of the Mediterranean Middle East.[52]

Today, the Western media depict Islamic societies such as Iran or Afghanistan under the Taliban as a fanatical merging of religious institutions with nation-states that is peculiar to Islam. But the history of Christianity, and the Catholic Church in particular, is one in which a similar merger occurred—in which the Church's immense wealth and power over European societies was broken only by bourgeois revolution in the eighteenth century.

The fact that Catholic morality, such as celibacy for priests—mandated in the eleventh century so the Church could inherit their property—stems mainly from the Middle Ages, yet continues to influence popular discourse in the twenty-first century is a testament to the Church's lasting influence in modern society. In colonial America, husbands were allowed to beat their wives—but not on Sundays or after 8:00 p.m., to avoid disturbing the peace. Not until 1911 did all U.S. states (except Mississippi) outlaw wife beating. Until 1973, English law permitted husbands to restrain their wives if they attempted to leave. Fathers still "give away" their daughters to their new husbands in Christian marriage, and in some U.S. states it is still legal for husbands to rape their wives.[53]

Both Christianity and Islam developed as a product of class society, and their ideologies flourished as a justification for the forms of class exploitation and women's oppression specific to the Middle Ages. But these ideologies live on in various forms in modern class society—and will retain their relevance as long as class exploitation and women's oppression continue to exist.

Marxism and religion

But religious ideology imposed from above would be meaningless without a mass of worshippers from below. As Karl Marx wrote in 1844, "Religious suffering is, at one and the same time, the expression of real suffering and a protest against real suffering. Religion is the sigh of the oppressed creature, the heart of a heartless world, and the soul of soulless conditions. It is the opium of the people."[54]

Religion acts as an ideological justification for the inequalities produced by class society, but is also a source of hope and comfort to many of those who are the most exploited and oppressed within class society. This theoretical understanding guided the practice of the Bolshevik Party, the revolutionary Marxists who eventually led the Russian working class to power in 1917.

The Russian revolutionary V.I. Lenin, was clear on both of these aspects of religion. "Marxism has always regarded all modern religions and churches, and each and every religious organization, as instruments of bourgeois reaction that serve to defend exploitation and to befuddle the working class."[55] But he also argued, echoing Marx, "Those who toil and live in want all their lives are taught by religion to be submissive and patient while here on earth, and to take comfort in the hope of a heavenly reward."[56]

For this reason, he argued in 1909,

No educational book can eradicate religion from the minds

of masses who are crushed by capitalist hard labor, and who are at the mercy of the blind destructive forces of capitalism, until those masses themselves learn to fight this *root* of religion, fight *the rule of capital* in all its forms, in a united, organized, planned and conscious way.[57]

The Bolsheviks were neither for outlawing religion nor condemning those who practiced religion, but rather regarded religion to be a purely "personal matter." As such, the party stood for the complete separation of church and state. Lenin wrote,

> Religion must be of no concern to the state, and religious societies must have no connection with governmental authority. Everyone must be absolutely free to profess any religion he pleases, or no religion whatever, i.c., to be an atheist, which every socialist is, as a rule. Discrimination among citizens on account of their religious convictions is wholly intolerable. Even the bare mention of a citizen's religion in official documents should unquestionably be eliminated. No subsidies should be granted to the established church nor state allowances made to ecclesiastical and religious societies.[58]

As Lenin notes, Marxism is based upon an understanding of historical materialism—and is therefore atheist. Nevertheless, the Bolshevik Party did not require atheism of its members, seeking instead to win those with religious beliefs over to the struggle to eliminate class society—the source and sustaining force of religion. Lenin argued, "We must not only admit workers who preserve their belief in God into the Social-Democratic Party, but must deliberately set out to recruit them; we are absolutely opposed to giving the slightest offense to their religious convictions, but we recruit them in order to educate them in the spirit of our program."[59]

In 1909, Lenin articulated a vision of post-revolutionary society entirely consistent with this patient approach:

> The revolutionary proletariat will succeed in making religion a really private affair, so far as the state is concerned. And in this political system, cleansed of medieval mildew, the proletariat will wage a broad and open struggle for the elimination of economic slavery, the true source of the religious humbugging of mankind.[60]

This materialist approach to religion instructed Bolshevik practice in the years immediately following the 1917 revolution, and should not be confused with the sharp break with the revolutionary Marxist tradition—and the extreme authoritarianism—that characterized the Stalinist counterrevolution a decade later.

The Russian Revolution

The conditions facing Russia's revolutionary government in 1917 were far from ideal for building a socialist society. Its factories were among the largest in the world, but as a whole the country remained economically backward. Its population was still some 80 percent peasantry spread across vast rural areas. Furthermore, its economy had been devastated by the First World War, and was soon to be further devastated by civil war, when fourteen counter-revolutionary armies backed by the Western powers invaded Russia in 1918, with the aim of overthrowing the young workers' state. For the next three years, the Bolsheviks were forced to use most of the country's deteriorating resources toward fighting a civil war, not building a socialist society.

And Tsarist Russia was an imperialist power in its own right. In 1917, just 43 percent of the Russian empire's population was Russian—the majority was made up of colonized peoples living in surrounding nations. If most of Russia itself was economically—and therefore culturally—backward, Russian imperialism had ensured that the vast Muslim regions of Central Asia were yet more so. As the Russian revolutionary Trotsky described, "Hierarchically organized exploitation, combining the barbarity of capitalism with the barbarity of patriarchal life, successfully held down the Asiatic peoples in extreme national abasement."[61]

From 1903, the Bolshevik platform incorporated the principle of the "right of self-determination for all nations included within the bounds of a state."[62] Lenin emphasized at all times that the

> self-determination of nations today *hinges* on the conduct of socialists in the oppressor nations. A socialist of any of the oppressor nations...who does not recognize and does not struggle for the right of oppressed nations to self-determination (i.e., the right to secession) is in reality a chauvinist, not a socialist.

And on November 2, 1917, the Russian revolutionary government, as one of its first acts, decreed the right of Russia's oppressed nations to self-determination up to secession and the formation of an independent state.[63]

Ending women's oppression was also central to the Bolshevik project. Like Marx and Engels before them, the Bolshevik leadership understood that women's role within the family, is the primary source of women's oppression. Therefore, removing household burdens from women was of the utmost priority for the Russian revolutionary government. Lenin argued in 1919,

> The real emancipation of women, real communism, will begin only where and when an all-out struggle begins (led by the proletariat wielding state power) against this petty housekeeping, or rather when it its wholesale transformation into a large-scale socialist economy begins…. Public catering establishments, nurseries, kindergartens—here we have examples of these shoots, here we have the simple, everyday means, involving nothing pompous, grandiloquent, or ceremonial, which can really emancipate women, really lessen and abolish their inequality with men as regards their role in social production and public life.[64]

But again, while one-third of Petrograd's factory workers were women in 1917, the vast majority of women lived far from cities, thoroughly oppressed and isolated in peasant communities heavily influenced by doctrines of Christianity in Russia, and in some cases pre-feudal communities dominated by Islam in the oppressed nations of Central Asia.[65]

As a general rule, the Bolsheviks approached the issue of religion as an ideology, in the revolutionary Marxist tradition outlined above. The revolutionary government did not seek to outlaw Christianity, Islam, Judaism, or any other religion. If religion is a product of the inequalities of class society, then ultimately its function should fade away in the absence of inequality, in a classless society. The point was not to persecute religious worshippers, but, in the first instance, to enact a firm separation between religious doctrine and civil law.

The revolutionary government enacted legislation establishing full social and political equality for women: the right to vote and to hold public office, the right to divorce at the request of either partner, the principle of equal pay for equal work, paid maternity leave for four months before and after childbirth, and child care at government expense. Abortion—viewed only as a health matter—was made legal in 1920, and women won the right to obtain free abortions in state hospitals. Only those who performed abortions for profit were considered criminals. In addition, the revolution repealed all laws criminalizing homosexuality and other laws regulating sexuality.[66]

But legal equality for oppressed groups was not enough. The Bolshevik leadership, Lenin in particular, forcefully argued that revolutionaries had a duty to struggle against sexist attitudes that continued to oppress women and also against the Russian colonial chauvinist prejudices against oppressed nationalities. German socialist Clara Zetkin recalled lengthy discussions with Lenin in 1920, where he argued,

Very few husbands, not even the proletarians, think of how much they could lighten the burdens and worries of their wives, or relieve them entirely, if they lent a hand in this "women's work".... Our Communist work among the masses of women, and our political work in general, involves considerable educational work among the men. We must root out the old slave-owner's point of view, both in the party and among the masses. That is one of our political tasks.[67]

Lenin was equally adamant in combating "Great Russian" chauvinism, as in this polemic against Joseph Stalin over the rights of the oppressed republic of Georgia in 1922:

Internationalism on the part of oppressors or "great" nations, as they are called (though they are great only in their violence, only great as bullies), must consist not only in the observance of the formal equality of nations but even in an inequality of the oppressor nation, the great nation, that must make up for the inequality which obtains in actual practice.... What is needed to ensure this? Not merely formal equality. In one way or another, by one's attitude or by concessions, it is necessary to compensate the non-Russian for the lack of trust, for the suspicion and the insults to which the government of the "dominant" nation subjected them in the past.[68]

This principled stance on national liberation should not be misconstrued as an endorsement of any religious ideology. Just as Lenin argued before the revolution, the state should approach religion as a "private matter," but the revolutionary party, based upon historical materialism, is atheist. The Bolsheviks were adamant that revolutionaries should make no concessions to the backward ideologies of any religion. The Comintern, the international movement of revolutionary parties set up by the Bolsheviks in 1919, adopted the following statement as part of its "Theses on the National and Colonial Question" in 1922: "An unconditional struggle must be carried out against the reactionary and medieval influence of the clergy, the Christian missions and similar elements." Another statement read: "A struggle is necessary against Panislamism, the Panasiatic movement and similar currents which try to tie the liberation struggle against European and American imperialism to the strengthening of the power of Turkish and Japanese imperialism, the nobility, the big landlords, the clergy, etc."[69]

Islam, national liberation, and women in revolutionary Russia

The need to rectify the colonial injustices of Tsarist Russia came into conflict with the goal of championing women's liberation, however, precisely on the issue of Islam. In many respects, the Bolshevik approach to Islam was the same as toward the Russian Orthodox Church, because women themselves have to be the agents in their own liberation rather than imposing liberation from above. But whereas Christianity was the religion favored in Russia, the oppressor nation, Islam was the religion of many of those oppressed by Tsarist Russia.

Russian imperialism had not merely prevented entire populations from advancing economically and politically, but suppressed their rights to speak their own languages or practice their own religions and cultures. As Leon Trotsky described, "The peoples and tribes along the Volga, in the northern Caucasus, in Central Asia...the struggle here was about matters like having their own alphabet, their own teachers—even at times their own priests."

Russian colonialism, like its European counterparts, was openly racist toward Muslims and hostile to Islamic culture. But Islam was, in turn, oppressive to women. By the end of 1922, seven of the USSR's eight autonomous republics were populated mainly by Muslims.[70] If autonomy were to be meaningful, Russian laws granting women equality could not be imposed from above. Public opinion had to be won over from below, through patient argument.

In 1919, the Bolsheviks created a party women's bureau, the Zhenotdel, under the direction of Inessa Armand, and, after her death in 1920, by Alexandra Kollontai. The Zhenotdel—whose motto, coined by Kollontai, came to be "agitation by deed"—was responsible for organizing communal kitchens, nurseries, and laundries that could begin to free working and peasant women of the burdens of housework. Developing an idea of Armand's, Zhenotdel agitators organized "delegates' assemblies," in which women were elected from factories and villages to work in apprenticeships running factories or hospitals, to serve in the soviets or unions, or even to function as administrators or judges.[71]

In the Zhenotdel's second year, 853 conferences of working and peasant women were held throughout Russia. By the mid-1920s, over 500,000 women had attended as conference delegates.[72] In the revolution's early years, the Zhenotdel took up a variety of campaigns, from support for the Red Army in the civil war to the promotion of education and literacy for women, with the aim of involving ever larger numbers of women.

Islamic customs, of course, varied from region to region. For example, in the regions that today are called Uzbekistan and Tajikistan—where the economies were based on settled agriculture—women were veiled and secluded within the home and prohibited from speaking to men other than relatives. But women in Turkmenistan—and other nomadic societies of Central Asia—were neither secluded nor veiled.[73]

Lacking local Bolsheviks to begin working among Muslim women, teams of Russian Zhenotdel organizers quietly began to meet with Muslim women to discuss women's rights and socialism, make crafts, and offer literacy instruction. When necessary, Zhenotdel organizers wore veils to avoid attracting attention because they frequently encountered hostility throughout Central Asia. On occasion, Zhenotdel workers and Muslim women members were attacked or killed by men hostile to changing women's status. (It should be noted, however, that a similar degree of hostility also existed in remote Christian areas, such as Ukraine.) In some Central Asian localities, however, the Zhenotdel was able to build up local organizations of Muslim women.[74]

But there were enormous obstacles to overcome before the ground could be prepared socially and economically for genuine reform. Unfortunately, as Joseph Stalin consolidated his power within the bureaucracy, he proved this point all too clearly. During the second half of the 1920s, after Lenin's death, Stalin began to outlaw so-called crimes of custom throughout Central Asia. One such crime of custom was the practice of paying "bridewealth" (*galing*)—payment from the groom's family to the bride's parents in marriage, often when the bride was very young. To be sure, this practice is a form of "selling" women. But bridewealth was central to an elaborate kinship network on which social structures were based. In Turkmenistan, for example, banning this custom was widely opposed. Bridewealth could not be simply "outlawed." It had to be replaced by an entirely different form of social organization.

Perhaps most importantly, however, the Russian state had no right to impose its rule on any question in Russia's former colonies. In so doing, Stalin betrayed the very principles of national liberation that were a hallmark of the Bolshevik tradition.

Too many historians blur the crucial distinction between Lenin and Stalin—and note without comment, for example, that the Zhenotdel developed a campaign in which Muslim women ceremoniously tore off their veils on International

Women's Day and May Day in Central Asia. That campaign reached its peak from 1927 to 1929—Stalin's ultra-left "third period" that accompanied the forced collectivization of agriculture. The unveilings were followed by the slaughter of many of the Muslim women who had participated by enraged husbands and brothers. In one quarter of 1929 alone, some 300 women were murdered in Central Asia.[75]

Like the ban on "crimes of custom," the campaign against the veil was a product of Stalin's increasing control, solidified in 1928, with a devastating impact on the oppressed nationalities—and women.

If the precondition for women's equality in Russia was to address its economic backwardness, this was yet more the case in Russia's former colonies, where imperialism had prevented any new development of the forces of production. The Bolsheviks who led the 1917 Revolution understood this. As Trotsky asserted, "The fate of the colonial possessions, especially in central Asia, would change together with the industrial evolution of the center."[76] The Comintern's "Theses on the National and Colonial Question" stated:

> From the principles set forth it follows that the whole policy of the Communist International on the national and colonial question must be based mainly on the union of the workers and toiling masses of all nations and countries in the common revolutionary struggle for the overthrow of the landlords and of the bourgeoisie. For only such a union can secure victory over capitalism, without which the destruction of national oppression and inequality is impossible.[77]

The rise of Stalinism overturned the theoretical foundations of the Bolshevik Revolution. In 1930, not long after outlawing "crimes of custom" in the name of women's equality, Stalin's regime dissolved the Zhenotdel. During the 1930s, abortion was outlawed, divorce became much more difficult, and Stalin proclaimed the "New Soviet Family," which meant the old "bourgeois family" with a new name.

Nevertheless, the early years of the Russian Revolution offer a glimpse, albeit rudimentary, of the potential for a socialist society to liberate all of humanity. Trotsky wrote, "Political practice remained, of course, far more primitive than political theory. For things are harder to change than ideas."[78] This would have been true in any case, but any honest assessment of the Bolsheviks' accomplishments must also take into account that the revolution was hamstrung by the conditions of civil war, while disease and famine plagued all parts of society. In this context, the revolution succeeded remarkably in combating oppression in all its forms.

The Bolsheviks, as leaders of the world revolutionary movement in the years immediately after 1917, built a movement that truly was, in Lenin's words, a "tribune of the people."[79] A speech given by Nadzhiya, a Turkish woman representative at the Baku Congress of the Peoples of the East in 1920, offers insight into the demands women in Muslim societies might put forward in the fight against their own oppression:

The women's movement beginning in the East must not be looked at from the standpoint of those frivolous feminists who are content to see woman's place in social life as that of a delicate plant or an elegant doll. This movement must be seen as a serious and necessary consequence of the revolutionary movement which is taking place throughout the world. The women of the East are not merely fighting for the right to walk in the street without wearing the chadra [veil], as many people suppose. For the women of the East, with their high moral ideals, the question of the chadra, it can be said, is of the least importance...

The women Communists of the East have an even harder battle to wage because, in addition, they have to fight against the despotism of their menfolk. If you, men of the East, continue now, as in the past, to be indifferent to the fate of women, you can be sure that our countries will perish, and you and us together with them: the alternative is for us to begin, together with all the oppressed, a bloody life-and-death struggle to win our rights by force. I will briefly set forth the women's demands. If you want to bring about your own emancipation, listen to our demands and render us real help and co-operation.

1) Complete equality of rights.

2) Ensuring for women unconditional opportunity to make use of the educational and vocational-training institutions established for men.

3) Equality of rights of both parties to marriage. Unconditional abolition of polygamy.

4) Unconditional admission of women to employment in legislative and administrative institutions.

5) Everywhere, in cities, towns and villages, committees for the rights and protection of women to be established.

Undoubtedly we can ask for all of this. The Communists,

recognizing that we have equal rights, have reached out their hand to us, and we women will prove their most loyal comrades. True, we may be stumbling in pathless darkness, we may be standing on the brink of yawning chasms, but we are not afraid, because we know that in order to see the dawn one has to pass through the dark night.[80]

Conclusion: Past and present

Although the possibilities of the revolutionary Marxist tradition have yet to be realized, its potential to combat both national and women's oppression can be seen in embryonic form in the Russian Revolution. The need to combat women's oppression was not counterposed to the fight against national oppression, for the elimination of both required the transition to a classless society. This, along with a clear understanding of the role of Islam as a religious doctrine that both sanctions the inequalities produced by class society—notably, women's oppression—and as an aspect of national culture brutally suppressed by imperialism in oppressed nations, offers lasting theoretical clarity.

The resurgence of Islam at the end of the twentieth century had its origin in the aims of American imperialism in the post–Cold War era—with a rise in racism toward Muslims parallel to the era of colonialism one hundred years earlier. The events of September 11 only accelerated this trend.

At the same time, neither imperialism nor its Islamic opposition can effectively address the issue of women's oppression, because both defend it in different forms. Leila Ahmed, assessing the colonialists and the Islamic movement nearly one hundred years ago, remarked, "For neither side was male dominance ever in question."[81] Elsewhere, she argues, "The resemblance between the two positions is not coincidental: they are mirror images of each other."[82] The solution to women's oppression—and imperialism—lies in the revolutionary Marxist tradition.

CHAPTER 5

Women and Socialism

FROM THEIR earliest writings, Karl Marx and Frederick Engels integrated an analysis of women's oppression as a fundamental element of Marxist theory. In *The Communist Manifesto*, written in 1848, Marx and Engels argued that the ruling class oppresses women, relegating women to second-class citizenship in society. "The bourgeois sees in his wife a mere instrument of production.… He has not even a suspicion that the real point aimed at [by communists] is to do away with the status of women as mere instruments of production."[1]

This short statement contains within it the core elements of the Marxist theory of women's liberation, developed fully by Engels in his groundbreaking work, *The Origin of the Family, Private Property and the State*, and put into practice by revolutionaries during the Russian Revolution of 1917.[2]

Central to the Marxist theory of women's oppression is an understanding of the role of the nuclear family in class society—and more recently, in capitalist society—and women's subjugated role *within* the family. Women's oppression is a product of class society—but all women, regardless of their social class, are oppressed as women.

The question of class

Marxists and feminists share the goal of women's equality, and have fought side by side for many reforms, from the right to vote to abortion rights. But Marxism and feminism base themselves upon different theoretical foundations, dating back more than a century. Many feminists have objected to the Marxist understanding that the root of women's oppression lies in class society, arguing that this analysis systematically subordinates the importance of women's oppression to issues of class. Much of modern feminist theory on the subject of Marxism originated during the radicalization of the 1970s, when the U.S. Left grew significantly from the civil rights, antiwar, and women's and gay liberation movements.

"Second wave" feminism, as it is known, developed a number of separate, but often overlapping, wings—including "socialist-feminism," an attempt to combine Marxist and feminist theory—that is, a system of class exploitation and women's oppression. According to socialist-feminists, two parallel systems exist side by side: the patriarchy, a system of male power, responsible for women's oppression, and capitalism, responsible for exploitation of the entire working class, including women workers. But this analysis was contradictory, and its popularity short-lived.

Women and Revolution: The Unhappy Marriage of Marxism and Feminism, published in 1981, summed up the frustrations of those trying to integrate the two analyses: "Either we need a happier marriage or we need a divorce." As one of the book's authors, Heidi Hartmann, argued,

> How are we to recognize patriarchal social relations in capitalist societies? It appears as if each woman is oppressed by her own man alone; her oppression seems a private affair....It is hard to recognize relationships among men, and between men and women, as *systemically* patriarchal. We argue, however, that a patriarchy as a system of relations between men and women exists in capitalism, and...a healthy and strong partnership exists between patriarchy and capital.

Hartmann concludes, "the struggle between men and women will have to continue along with the struggle against capital."[3]

However appealing this theory sounded in the abstract, the theory of a separate system of patriarchy crumbled when confronted with the possibility of broad-based struggle. It is not possible for working-class women to simultaneously unite with working-class men in the class struggle and to unite with ruling-class women in the struggle against working-class men, as part of the patriarchy. If there is a system of male power—that is, a partnership between working-class men and the capitalist class—the possibility of class struggle is undermined. On the other hand, if ruling-class women and their maids are to unite against the patriarchy (of all classes), what would be their unifying demands? Concretely, either class or gender must dominate; either the working class will unite against capital or women of all classes will unite against men of all classes.

History has shown that when the class interests of upper-class and working-class women collide, "sisterhood" does not cross class lines. This quickly became apparent when working-class women, in the aftermath of the women's liberation movement of the 1970s, began to demand maternity leave, and found middle-class feminist organizations, such as the National Organization for Women (NOW) and the women's section of the American Civil Liberties Union (ACLU), completely opposed.

In 1978, these organizations rushed to submit legal briefs *against* the right to maternity leave, in the case of *California Federal Savings and Loan v. Guerra*. It all began when a bank employee—a single mother—took six months off after a complicated pregnancy. When she returned to work, she found out she had been fired from her job. The bank decided to use the incident as a test case to strike down a 1978 California law entitling women workers to pregnancy or maternity leave, on the grounds that it "discriminates" against men with similar "disabilities" (despite the obvious biological impossibility). The argument made by middle-class feminists, in the words of the ACLU's Joan Berton, was this: "The question is, should a woman with a pregnancy disability get her job back when other employees with disabilities get fired? You undermine your argument unless you say everyone is equally entitled to this benefit."[4]

Why would a feminist organization oppose the right to maternity leave for women workers? Middle-class feminist organizations reflect the class interests of their membership—the growing number of women professionals and executives. These women do not need special reforms to help them fulfill their family responsibilities because they have the wealth to hire others (usually working-class women) to carry out the bulk of domestic and child care tasks. On the contrary, they wish to play down the differences between themselves and their male corporate counterparts, which have been used to deny women executive positions.

Working-class women, however, have no way around the responsibility imposed by children and familial commitments. Every reform that helps to lessen the burden of oppression for women workers—be it maternity leave, abortion, or child care services—is a welcome one. That is why these sorts of "special demands" have been raised repeatedly within the working-class movement. Maternity leave is a class question, not a feminist issue. The *California Federal Savings* case showed clearly how a victory for the women of one class can be a setback for women of another class.

Marxism and women's oppression

The revolutionary Marxist tradition, while locating the source of women's oppression in class society, encompasses a full appreciation of the magnitude of inequality existing between women and men of all classes in society, inside the family and in society as a whole. As the Russian revolutionary leader Leon Trotsky wrote, "In order to change the conditions of life, we must learn to see them through the eyes of women." Furthermore, Trotsky argued,

> to achieve the actual equality of man and woman within the family is an...arduous problem. All our domestic habits must be revolutionized before that can happen. And yet it is quite obvious that unless there is actual equality of husband and wife in the family, in a normal sense as well as in the conditions of life, we cannot speak seriously of their equality in social work or even in politics.[5]

It would be easy to conclude that because men and women are not treated as equals in society at large or within the family, even working-class men "benefit" from the oppression of women and exercise "male power" over women. If this logic is extended to other forms of oppression, then white, male, and heterosexual workers all "benefit" from racism, sexism, and homophobia. And all workers in advanced industrial societies with higher incomes benefit from the low wages of workers in poor countries.

The Marxist view is quite different. There is a crucial difference between not personally suffering from racism, sexism, and homophobia and objectively benefiting from these forms of special oppression. The working class as a whole suffers because of oppression, and has an objective interest in ending oppression in all its forms.

In fact, the working class as a whole is oppressed, as well as exploited. And the special oppression faced by women, gays, Blacks, and other racially oppressed parts of the population serves both to lower the living standards of the entire working class and to weaken workers' ability to fight back.

For example, corporate globalization has raised profits by lowering working class living standards throughout the world. Over the last thirty years, U.S. workers have been transformed from the highest paid in the world to among the lowest in advanced industrial societies as their wages have come into competition with those of low-wage economies. So, even in the short term, the working class from the richest countries has nothing to gain from oppression of workers in low-wage economies.

In Marx and Engels' time, there was little doubt that the working class suffered not only from exploitation, but also from oppression. Engels' book, *The Condition of the Working Class in England,* published in 1845, describes the extreme poverty of the British working class brought about by the industrial revolution. Living standards improved dramatically in advanced industrial societies in the last century. Nevertheless, even in the richest societies in the world, including the United States, the working class experiences oppression. Oppression takes many forms: regressive taxation policies; inferior working-class schools; substandard or inaccessible medical care; the prevailing ideologies, which teach workers that they are less intelligent or less capable than the better-educated middle and upper classes; even the siting of toxic waste dumps, never installed anywhere but in working-class areas—the list goes on and on.

Oppression is necessary to (and a product of) a system based upon the rule of a tiny minority at the expense of the vast majority. The special forms of oppression experienced by women, gays, Blacks, Latinos, Arabs, and other racial groups in society are also endemic to the system. Women's oppression rose hand in hand with the family, along with the development of class society.[6] Anti-gay ideology grew up as an ideological prop to legitimize the traditional heterosexual nuclear family.[7] Racism developed as a product of slavery.[8] Today these various forms of oppression serve to uphold the capitalist system in particular ways. But they also serve a more general function for capital: pitting worker against worker by creating divisions within the working class.

The ruling class deliberately fosters antagonisms between different sections of the working class by actively promoting inequality and discriminating against certain parts of the population. Using whatever means are at its disposal, including the legal system, the media, the educational system,

and prevailing ideologies, the ruling class creates scapegoats to blame for society's ills, or to be relegated to second-
class citizenship. Harmful stereotypes are made to seem like
"common sense." The prejudice that most women are too
"emotional" to be effective leaders and that most African
Americans are too "lazy" or "unintelligent" to succeed in professional careers goes a long way toward explaining the fact
that women and Blacks are grossly underrepresented in
Congress and there has never been a woman or African-
American president of the United States.

When the ruling class is most successful at fostering such
divisions, those groups who suffer the most from discrimination are also the most despised people in society. It is they,
not the system, who are blamed for society's problems. Marx
applied this theoretical approach to the role of racism and
slavery in the United States. He said, "In fact, the veiled slavery of the wage laborers in Europe needed the unqualified
slavery of the New World as its pedestal..." The Black aboli-
tionist Frederick Douglass summed up the purpose of racism
in this simple phrase, "They divided both to conquer each."[9]

The period after the introduction of the Jim Crow segregation laws in the South at the turn of the century illustrates
this dynamic perfectly. Far from benefiting from the extreme
level of racism brought about by Jim Crow, Southern white
workers earned wages lower than those of Black workers in
the North.[10] Whenever capitalists can threaten to replace one

group of workers with another poorly paid group of workers, neither group benefits. The only beneficiaries of this inequality are the ruling class, who pay lower wages overall.

The same relationship holds between the wages of men and those of women workers, which have never been close to equal. Women's wages in the United States now hover at roughly 75 percent of men's. But this has the net effect of depressing men's wages, for they are made constantly aware that if their own wage demands aim too high, they can be replaced with cheaper women workers. One hundred years ago, the occupation of clerical work was almost entirely made up of men. Today, clerical workers are overwhelmingly lower paid women workers. The effect of special oppression is to increase the level of oppression for the entire working class.

Indeed, this relationship has been borne out by the fluctuation between men's and women's wages over the last thirty years. Median workers' wages in the United States have fallen significantly since 1972. "Four out of five households take home a thinner slice of the economic pie than they did a quarter century before," according to labor historian Nelson Lichtenstein.[11] But during this same period, women's hourly wages have *risen* in relationship to men's—primarily because men's wages have been falling, not because women's wages have risen significantly. Women workers in 1979 earned, on average, just 59 cents for every dollar earned by men; today the figure is significantly higher, at 76 cents. But, as Lichtenstein

explains, "The decline in wages has been especially pro-
nounced among young male workers, whose real wages declined by 25 percent from the early 1970s to the early 1990s."[12]

The role of the family

The source of oppression for both women and gays involves another key feature of the capitalist system: the role of
the nuclear family. The nuclear family grew up hand in hand
with the development of class society. During the early flourishing of industrial capitalism low wages forced entire working-class families, including children, to labor in factories in
order to survive. This situation, however, severely undermined the working-class family to the point of threatening its
existence. Indeed, Marx and Engels (mistakenly) believed
that the working-class family was disappearing under capitalism. But from the mid-nineteenth century onwards, the trend
was toward consolidation of the family. Wages rose enough
so that more working-class women would remain within the
home and make child-rearing a priority.

The modern working-class family developed as part of
the superstructure of class society, alongside the legal system, the military and police, the educational system—and
the rest of the complex and intertwined structures that exist
to legitimize and uphold the inequalities inherent to class society, and more recently, to the capitalist mode of production—i.e., exploitation. On a purely material level, the family

functions to provide the system with a plentiful supply of labor. The working-class family developed as a cheap way (for capitalists, not for workers) to reproduce labor power, both in terms of replenishing the daily strength of the current labor force and also as a way of raising future generations of workers through adulthood.

Capitalists have come to rely upon "privatized reproduction," as Marx called it, in which nearly the entire financial burden for raising children and household maintenance belongs to individual working-class family units—reliant primarily upon one or two parents' wages for survival—rather than government expenditure. This burden is even more extreme in the United States compared with other advanced industrial economies that offer universal health care, paid parental leave, and other government benefits to individual families.

While it might have been possible for capitalism to develop without relying on the family and privatized reproduction, it is doubtful at this point that capitalism could do without—or that capitalists would be willing to do without—the institution of the nuclear family. In 1995, the United Nations Development Program reported that women's unpaid and underpaid labor amounted to $11 trillion worldwide—and $1.4 trillion in the United States each year.[13]

Engels argued that the role of the "proletarian wife" meant "the wife became the head servant...if she carries out her duties in the private service of her family, she remains excluded from public production and unable to earn; and if she wants to take part in public production and earn independently, she cannot carry out her family duties."[14] To this day, the competing demands of job and family are a major source of stress for all working mothers—but are especially so in working-class families, who cannot afford to hire others to help with laundry, housework, cooking, and other domestic chores.

In order to prop up the family, ruling-class ideology compels both women and men to adhere to rigidly demarcated sex roles—the ideal of homemaker for women, subordinate to the family's male breadwinner—regardless of how little these ideals actually reflect the real lives of working-class people. Since the 1970s, the vast majority of women have been part of the labor force, yet these family ideals—and the assumption that women are better suited to domestic responsibilities within the family—live on. Women's caretaking role inside the family reduces their status to second-class citizens in society as a whole, because their primary responsibility—and greatest contribution—is assumed to be servicing their individual families' needs.

An essential component of bourgeois ideology legitimizing the family is the portrayal of human sexuality as "naturally" or "normally" heterosexual. Ideal men are portrayed as "daring" and "brave," while women are encouraged to be "nurturing" and "pleasing" to men. The ideal nuclear family encompasses the lifelong committment between this "brave" breadwinner, his "nurturing" wife, and their offspring.

Those who do not adhere to this rigid standard—divorced and single parents, and gays in particular—are labeled "abnormal." This aspect of the ideology of the family is so essential that the very existence of lesbians and gays who choose to live outside the traditional heterosexual nuclear family poses a threat. Laws governing sexual behavior and explicitly defining homosexuality as deviant began to appear well into the development of capitalism, in the late nineteenth century. As Sherry Wolf described,

> Reams of historical evidence confirm that homosexual behavior has existed for at least thousands of years, and it's logical to assume that homosexual acts have been going on for as long as human beings have walked the earth. But only when capitalist society in the late-nineteenth century created the potential for individuals to live outside the nuclear family, was the modern conception of a gay identity born.[15]

Who benefits?

It is crucial to understand the family's role in privatized reproduction for capitalism. Otherwise, it can seem as if the personal relationships that exist inside the family produce oppression by themselves—particularly for women. Inequality between women and men exists within virtually every family, because women typically take much more responsibility for housework and child care than men, and women remain widely viewed as subordinates to their husbands. But the unpaid labor women perform inside the family is labor that benefits only the ruling class. Working-class men have no objective interest in maintaining the role of the nuclear family as it exists under capitalism, for it places the entire financial burden of reproduction on the shoulders of working-class men and women. Working-class men also have an interest in fighting for a system in which housework is socialized and quality child care is available whenever it is needed.

This viewpoint was long ago rejected by second wave radical feminists who regarded a system of "male power" as the source and main beneficiary of women's oppression. Susan Brownmiller, for example, stated in her classic book, *Against Our Will: Men, Women and Rape:*

> When men discovered that they could rape, they proceeded to do it…. Man's discovery that his genitalia could serve as a weapon to generate fear must rank as one of the most important discoveries of prehistoric times, along with the use of fire and the first crude stone axe. From prehistoric times to the present, I believe, rape has played a critical function. It is nothing more and nothing less than a conscious process by which *all men* keep *all women* in a state of fear. [Italicized in original.][16]

Not surprisingly, Brownmiller is thoroughly disparaging of Marxism, dismissing its importance in a mere paragraph: "And the great socialist theoreticians Marx and Engels and their many confreres and disciples who developed the theory of class oppression and put words like 'exploitation' into the everyday vocabulary, they, too were strangely silent about rape, unable to fit it into their economic constructs."[17]

But Brownmiller does not merely (inaccurately) accuse Marxists of systematically underestimating the importance or degree of the personal aspects of women's oppression, rape in particular. Rather, she counterposes the root of all inequality in society as originating with male power over women:

> It seems eminently sensible to hypothesize that man's violent capture and rape of the female led first to the establishment of a rudimentary mate-protectorate and then sometime later to the full-blown solidification of power, the patriarchy. As the first permanent acquisition of man, his first piece of real property, woman was, in fact, the cornerstone, of the "house of the father." Man's forcible extension of his boundaries to his mate and later to their offspring was the beginning of the concept of ownership. Concepts of hierarchy, slavery and private property flowed from, and could only be predicated upon, the initial subjugation of women."

The Marxist view locates the source of women's oppression as flowing from the needs of class society—and, significantly, coming into existence alongside the development of inequality and class exploitation. This does not mean that Marxists disregard the personal aspects of women's oppression or any other form of oppression. On the contrary, Engels emphasized the extreme degradation suffered by women at the hands of their husbands, unknown in pre-class societies, calling it "the world historic defeat of the female sex." Moreover, Engels explicitly argued, as the following passage shows, that rape and violence against women were features of women's oppression within the family.

> The man took command in the home also; the woman was
> degraded and reduced to servitude; she became the slave of
> his lust and a mere instrument for the production of chil-
> dren…. In order to make certain of the wife's fidelity and
> therefore the paternity of his children, she is delivered over
> unconditionally into the power of the husband; if he kills her,
> he is only exercising his rights.[18]

However, Engels understood that the nuclear family was a
consequence—not the cause, as Brownmiller argued—of exploitation inherent to class society. Furthermore, class differences between women prevent them from sharing common
interests. The inequality suffered by women within landhold-
ing families, as described by Engels above—whose estates
relied upon the labor of serfs or slaves—was necessarily of a
different character than that of women serfs and slaves, and
in modern capitalism, women workers. Historically, ruling-
class women have been systematically denied a role in production, trapped exclusively in the household domain, while
women who are serfs, slaves, or workers suffer as laborers,
within a family who also suffer as laborers. While the wealthy
"trophy wife" undoubtedly suffers from oppression, the
woman laborer is subject not only to women's oppression,
but class exploitation, alongside her entire family.

Furthermore, while women's oppression may have its origin in women's role inside the family, women's second-class
status is system-wide. Women are discriminated against in all

realms of society. Even the Equal Rights Amendment (ERA), offering legal equality to women, has wallowed without passage for three decades. Women are reduced to sexual commodities on television and film, earn lower wages than men, are deprived of adequate and affordable child care and medical care, and are deprived of access to affordable abortion. Women's oppression is endemic to capitalism.

The reality of life inside individual families varies in quality, but rarely matches the social ideal of lifetime marital bliss and nurturing fulfillment for all. Many families become places where frustrations are acted upon, verbally and sometimes physically, especially in times of unemployment and other periods of financial or emotional duress. Child beating, incest, and other forms of abuse, as well as wife beating, are more common than officially acknowledged, since they are often kept as family secrets.

Most men hold sexist ideas and prejudices, but many women also share these sexist ideas. To be sure, some men beat and rape women, but most men do not. And many men support and have actively fought for the ERA, equal pay, and abortion rights for women. These enormous variations in individual consciousness—among both men and women—provide evidence that women's oppression is not the product of a unique system of "male power." Sexism, in all its forms, however brutal—like racism and homophobia—represents aspects of "false consciousness," as Marx described—of holding ideas that work against one's own class interests.

Since Marx and Engels, Marxists have understood that privatized reproduction through the nuclear family must be ended in order to end women's oppression and to create the material conditions in which women and men can truly become equals in their personal lives. Engels himself said, in a passage from *The Origin of the Family, Private Property and the State*:

> What we can now conjecture about the way in which sexual relations will be ordered after the impending overthrow of capitalist production is mainly of a negative character, limited for the most part to what will disappear. But what will there be new? That will be answered when a new generation has grown up: a generation of men who never in their lives have known what it is to buy a woman's surrender with money or any other social instrument of power; a generation of women who have never known what it is to give themselves to a man from any other considerations than real love or to refuse to give themselves to their lover from fear of the economic consequences.[19]

Rather than downplaying women's oppression, the emphasis by Marxists on the source of oppression leads to the conclusion that class society must be overthrown in order to create the possibility of ending it. Moreover, understanding oppression as a necessary function of class society—which benefits capitalists, not workers—explains why the entire working class has an interest in ending oppression in all its forms.

Why the working class can end women's oppression

One of the biggest myths about the U.S. working class is that it is made up primarily of white men. In reality, the working class includes people of all races and both genders (white male workers are actually a minority of all workers today) working not only in factories and on construction sites, but in offices, hospitals, airlines, restaurants, department stores, supermarkets, and classrooms. In fact, the majority of working people in the United States are part of the working class.[20]

In the context of capitalism, the working class is the revolutionary class in society—whom Marx described as capitalism's "gravediggers." The working class holds the potential to lead a struggle in the interests of all those who suffer injustice and oppression. That is because both exploitation and oppression are rooted in class society. Exploitation is the method by which the ruling class robs workers of the products of their labor. But various forms of oppression play a primary role in maintaining the rule of a tiny minority over the vast majority.

But when Marx defined the working class as the agent for revolutionary change, he was describing its historical potential, rather than a foregone conclusion. While capitalism propels workers toward collective forms of struggle, it also forces them into competition. The unremitting pressure from a layer of unemployed workers, which exists in most economies even in times of "full employment," is a deterrent to struggle—a constant reminder that workers compete for a limited number of jobs that afford a decent standard of living.

Without the counterweight of class struggle, and the class solidarity that is a product of struggle, this competition can act as an obstacle to the development of class consciousness, encouraging the growth of false consciousness—and a rise in prejudices and bigotry that divide workers and impede their ability to focus on the real enemy. For example, racism against immigrants can grow in times of high unemployment, undermining workers' ability to build a united fightback against unemployment. Bourgeois ideology may serve to benefit only the ruling class, but it affects all classes in society, including the working class.

However, the dynamic is such that workers' objective circumstances are always in conflict with bourgeois ideology. Marx and Engels argued in *The Communist Manifesto,* "This organization of proletarians into a class, and consequently into a political party, is continually being upset again by the competition between the workers themselves. But it ever rises up again, stronger, firmer, mightier."[21]

Marx distinguished between a working class "in itself," which holds objective revolutionary potential, and a working class "for itself," which acts in its own class interests. The difference is between the objective potential and the subjective organization needed to realize that potential. An essential part of this process is the development of political consciousness among workers.

The role played by organized revolutionaries can be crucial to the development of political consciousness among workers. A battle of ideas must be fought inside the working class movement. The experience of the 1917 Russian Revolution showed how a section of workers, already won to a socialist alternative and organized into a revolutionary party, can win other workers away from false consciousness by providing an alternative world view. The Russian revolutionary V.I. Lenin helped to advance the Marxist theory of the revolutionary party, based upon the Bolshevik Party's experiences during the decades that preceded the 1917 revolution.

For Lenin, the goal of political consciousness required workers' willingness to champion the interests of all the oppressed in society, as a part of the struggle for socialism: "Working class consciousness cannot be genuine political consciousness unless the workers are trained to respond to *all* cases of tyranny, oppression, violence, and abuse, no matter *what class is* affected—unless they are trained, moreover, to respond from a Social-Democratic point of view and no other."[22]

Class provides a unifying basis for fighting against oppression. Only a movement organized on the basis of genuine solidarity between all who are exploited and oppressed by capitalism holds the potential to wipe out oppression in all its forms. Far from ignoring oppression, the Marxist view is that the working class cannot hope to win a socialist society *unless* the working class movement is united on the basis of ending all forms of oppression and exploitation. Thus, it is in workers' objective interests to fight oppression in all its forms. The Leninist conception of the revolutionary party is that it always represents the objective interests of the working class, and on this basis argues within the working class movement that the socialist movement must, in Lenin's words, be the "tribune of the people."[23]

Women and the Russian Revolution

The 1917 Russian Revolution was a working-class revolution, built from below. Yet even in the economically backward country that Russia was in 1917—devastated by world war, and soon to be further devastated by civil war—the Bolshevik revolution succeeded remarkably in laying the early groundwork for constructing a genuinely democratic society run by workers themselves, governing through workers' councils, or *soviets*.[24]

The Russian Revolution of 1917 achieved the greatest advance toward women's liberation since class society arose. Many of the rights granted to women by Russia's revolutionary government have yet to be won in the most advanced industrial societies of the twenty-first century. This was no accident, but the result of ongoing commitment to winning equality for women. In the years of building a socialist organization in Russia before 1917, the Bolshevik Party learned how to build a movement for working-class power that integrated the special demands and needs of women and other specially oppressed parts of the population.

At the turn of the century, women already made up a large section of the Russian labor force. By the First World War, women were one-third of the workforce, and by 1917, they represented one-half.[25] Moreover, Russian women were never a docile section of workers, already making themselves heard on the picket lines, often leading strikes of their own demanding maternity leave, time off from work to nurse their babies, or an end to sexual harassment and bullying from their supervisors.[26]

Alexandra Kollontai was a long-standing Russian Marxist who joined the Bolshevik Party in 1915 over shared opposition to the First World War. She played a prominent leadership role throughout 1917, both within the *soviets* and as a leader of the Bolshevik Party. After the revolution, Kollontai was elected Commissar of Social Welfare by the Second All-Russian Congress of Soviets. Kollontai spearheaded the Bolshevik Party's approach to what was then called "the woman question," and developed key elements of modern Marxist theory and practice on the relationship between women's liberation and the general working-class struggle.[27]

Kollontai was keenly aware that women workers played a very militant role in the 1905 revolutionary upsurge in Russia, but their militancy did not translate into either trade union or political party membership on any large scale. Statistics reflect the very low level of participation among Russian women in political and trade union organizations. As late as 1922, Russian women made up only 22.2 percent of the union membership. In 1924, even after major efforts to recruit women workers into the party, women's membership in the Bolsheviks stood at only 8.2 percent.[28]

Kollontai emphasized that the combination of poverty, long work hours, and family responsibilities made it difficult for Russian women workers and peasants to participate in political activity, and she concluded that revolutionaries needed to make special efforts and develop new methods of reaching out to women workers in order to involve them in the struggle for a new society.

The class divide

Kollontai's approach to organizing among women was based upon class as well as gender. Beginning in 1906, following the lead of German socialists, Kollontai began to actively organize a working women's movement—as a distinct alternative to the middle-class, or "bourgeois," feminist movement. The middle-class Russian feminists, who concentrated their efforts on winning women's right to vote, emphasized the common interest shared by women of all classes in the drive for suffrage—and urged working-class women to submerge their class demands in a united women's movement. However, women workers immediately encountered antagonism from the "fine ladies" of the suffragette movement when they attempted to raise their own class demands. As Kollontai described in her book, *Towards a History of the Working Women's Movement in Russia*:

> Women's meetings were especially numerous during 1905 and 1906. Working women attended them willingly; they listened attentively to the bourgeois feminists but did not respond with much enthusiasm, since the speakers gave no suggestion as to how the urgent problems of those enslaved by capital might be solved. The women of the working class suffered from the harsh conditions at work, from hunger and insecurity. Their most urgent demands were: a shorter working day, higher wages, more human treatment from the factory authorities, less police supervision and more scope for "independent action." Such needs were foreign to the bourgeois feminists…
>
> During 1905 the bourgeois feminists in St. Petersburg and Moscow took the initiative in organizing the first meeting for servants. The response was encouraging and the first meetings were well attended, but when the "Union for Women's Equality" tried to organize servants according to its formula of an idyllic union of lady employers and their employees, the servants turned away and, to the chagrin of the feminists, transferred themselves rapidly to the party of their class, organizing their own special trade unions.[29]

In 1908, when the first All-Russian Congress of Women was called, Kollontai and the socialists organized a contingent of forty-five working women, who argued against the strategy of "classless unity" among women in the fight for women's liberation. They staged a walkout in protest against the bourgeois feminists. In preparation for this conference,

Kollontai wrote what would become a defining contribution to Marxist theory on women's liberation, "The Social Basis of the Woman Question"—in which she spelled out why there could be no genuine alliance between working-class and ruling-class women. She wrote:

> The women's world is divided, just as is the world of men, into two camps: the interests and aspirations of one group bring it close to the bourgeois class, while the other group has close connections to the proletariat, and its claims for liberation encompass a full solution to the woman question. Thus, although both camps follow the general slogan of the "liberation of women," their aims and interests are different. Each of the groups unconsciously takes its starting point from the interests and aspirations of its own class, which gives a specific class coloring to the targets and tasks it sets for itself…however apparently radical the demands of the feminists, one must not lose sight of the fact that the feminists cannot, on account of their class position, fight for that fundamental transformation of society, without which the liberation of women cannot be complete.[30]

International Women's Day, designated as an official socialist holiday by the Copenhagen Conference of Socialist Women in 1910, was first celebrated in Russia in 1913. But, because of massive police repression, the Bolsheviks were forced to celebrate under the guise of "a scientific morning devoted to the woman question." Nevertheless, the holiday was celebrated in five cities in Russia in 1913, and in the years of the First World War leading up to 1917, was celebrated by "flash meetings" designed to assemble and disperse quickly, to avoid police interference.[31]

In 1914, the Bolshevik leadership became convinced that a newspaper to reach out to women workers was necessary. To that end, the *Woman Worker,* or *Rabotnitsa,* was created. The party published seven issues. Police confiscated more than one full issue before the First World War broke out, and production was halted. Although the success of the women's newspaper was limited, it helped to develop a link between socialist organizers and small groups of workers. More importantly, it helped to develop a practice and priority of orienting specifically to women workers.[32]

The outbreak of the First World War brought about a short-lived, but devastating, whirlwind of patriotism in all the "belligerent" countries. Patriotism became the dividing question within the socialist movement itself, as entire socialist parties plunged themselves into the war efforts of their "own" ruling classes. If the divisions between revolutionary socialists and bourgeois feminists had ever seemed unclear before, they burst into full view during the war. Ruling-class women threw themselves into the war effort as a trade-off— in return, they demanded voting rights. The League for Women's Equality, for example, called on Russian women to "devote all our energy, intellect, and knowledge to our country. This is our obligation to our fatherland, and this will give us the right to participate as the equals of men in the new life of a victorious Russia."[33]

For the first nine months of the war, the labor movement in Russia ground to a halt, as workers went off to fight and die for their rulers. As the war dragged on, however, prices climbed and shortages of food plagued the cities and countryside. The war pulled many women into Russian industry. Thus, the number of women workers increased in Russia, and the types of jobs they held changed. Women flooded into formerly all-male industries like metal and lumber. Women became streetcar conductors and miners. By 1917, 50,000 of Petrograd's factory workers were women.[34]

However, the wages that women were paid for these jobs were far lower than those that men had received. Many, if not most, women were the sole supporters of their children during the war. In many cases, hunger drove women into action against the government. As early as April 1915, women rioted over shortages of bread and other staple foods. Increasingly, strikes, which began over economic grievances, generalized to incorporate political demands, such as an end to the war or the freeing of political prisoners.

Women and revolution

In February 1917, women textile workers in Petrograd organized a demonstration for International Women's Day under the theme "Opposition to the war, high prices, and the situation of the woman worker." The International Women's Day demonstration—the first mass celebration of the working women's holiday on Russian soil—resulted in a massive strike movement, which, in turn, overthrew the tsar. This day became, effectively, the first day of the Russian Revolution.

As one Russian observer described,

> If future historians look for the group that began the Russian Revolution, let them not create any involved theory. The Russian Revolution was begun by hungry women and children demanding bread and herrings. They started by wrecking tram cars and looting a few small shops. Only later did they, along with workmen and politicians, become ambitious to wreck that mighty edifice, the Russian aristocracy.[35]

At first, the Petrograd Bolsheviks underestimated the movement among the textile workers, urging them not to organize a mass demonstration for International Women's Day. But once the strike movement had spread to over 200,000 workers, the Bolsheviks understood the crucial role played by women workers. The Petrograd party branch initiated a Women's Bureau to help draw working women into political activity. In March 1917, the Bolsheviks reestablished the *Woman Worker,* with a circulation of 40,000 to 50,000. The party launched a working woman's school to train women workers as professional organizers. Bolshevik factory and district meetings addressed issues of interest to working women, including the eight-hour day and equal rights for women. All these efforts aimed to draw non-party women into political activity.[36] Bolshevik organizers joined women workers on the picket lines, arguing for the need for working-class power.

But the other side of the party's project involved an effort to convince working-class men of the need to support the demands of women workers. The Bolsheviks intervened in strikes and struggles involving a majority of male workers, arguing that working men's class interests lay in fighting for demands such as maternity protection and equal pay for women. Once again, Kollontai played a key role in developing the framework for this argument. In preparation for the First All-Russian Congress of Trade Unions in 1917, Kollontai called on working-class men to support equal pay for women workers:

> The class-conscious worker must understand that the value of male labor is dependent on the value of female labor, and that by threatening to replace male workers with cheaper female labor, the capitalist can put pressure on men's wages, lowering them to the level of women's wages. Therefore, only a lack of understanding could lead one to see the question of equal pay for equal work as purely a "woman's issue."[37]

The coalition government that assumed power after the tsar's overthrow in February 1917 became the "official" government of Russia, dedicated to returning to a stable class society. But a network of factory committees, workers' councils *(soviets)* and soldiers' committees earned the loyalty of a significant proportion of the working class, resulting in a situation of dual power—two parallel governments, one representing workers, the other, the status quo. This unstable situation could not last indefinitely. Eventually one class or the other would assume control over the whole of Russia. The Bolshevik Party stood consistently for the transfer of power to the soviets from the provisional government. As the war continued, and the provisional government continued to back it, the Bolsheviks won massive support among workers, soldiers, and peasants. Party membership swelled from 176,000 members in July 1917 to 260,000 members in early 1918. An estimated 10 percent of the industrial working class of Russia belonged to the Bolshevik Party by October 1917. More importantly, Bolshevik delegates won a majority among elected delegates to the soviets, reflecting majority support for insurrection.

The industrial working class clearly and unequivocally made the October Revolution. The Bolshevik-led insurrection overturned the provisional government and handed power over to the soviets. As an opponent of the Bolsheviks, the Menshevik Martov, wrote,

Understand, please, what we have before us after all is a victorious uprising of the proletariat—almost the entire proletariat supports Lenin and expects its social liberation from the uprising...[38]

Zhenotdel

Women were involved in nearly every aspect of the October Revolution, which embraced a full program for women's liberation. The October Revolution was indeed a "festival of the oppressed," as Trotsky described it. All of those oppressed and exploited in Tsarist Russia were liberated by the workers' government.

The revolutionary government enacted decrees that established full social and political equality for women: the right to vote and hold public office, the principle of equal pay for equal work, paid maternity leave for four months before and after childbirth and child care at government expense. By 1920, legislation was passed that regarded abortion simply as a health matter, and women won the right to obtain free abortions in state hospitals.

In addition, the revolution made great strides forward in combating other aspects of sexual discrimination. All laws criminalizing homosexuality were repealed, in an attempt to rid society of the distinction between gay and straight sexuality. The Bolshevik Grigorii Btakis described the impact of the October Revolution on sexuality in 1923:

> [Soviet legislation] declares the absolute non-interference of the state and society into sexual matters, so long as nobody is injured, and no one's interests are encroached upon—concerning homosexuality, sodomy, and various other forms of sexual gratification, which are set down in European legislation as offences against morality—Soviet legislation treats these exactly as so-called "natural" intercourse.[39]

But legal equality was only the beginning. As Lenin explained in 1919,

> Laws alone are not enough, and we are by no means content with mere decrees. In the sphere of legislation, however, we have done everything required of us to put women in a posi-

tion of equality and we have every right to be proud of it. The position of women in Soviet Russia is now ideal as compared with their position in the most advanced states. We tell ourselves, however, that this, of course, is only the beginning.[40]

Like Marx and Engels before them, the Bolshevik leadership understood that a woman's role within the family, which Lenin called "household slavery," lies at the root of women's oppression. The conditions of extreme deprivation facing Russia were made yet worse when fourteen counterrevolutionary armies—backed by the Western powers, including the United States—invaded Russia in 1918, with the aim of overthrowing the new workers' state. For the next three years, the Bolsheviks were forced to use the country's deteriorating resources toward fighting a civil war, not building a socialist society. In these dire circumstances, the workers' government nevertheless made real strides in setting up socialized restaurants, nurseries, and laundries, allowing more women the time and energy to participate, for the first time, as full citizens and to take on new roles in running their workplaces and government. As Lenin argued in a 1919 pamphlet,

> Notwithstanding all the laws emancipating women, she continues to be a domestic slave, because petty housework crushes, strangles, stultifies and degrades her, chains her to the nursery, and she wastes her labor on barbarously unproductive, petty, nerve-racking, stultifying and crushing drudgery. The real emancipation of women, real communism, will begin only where and when an all-out struggle begins (led by the proletariat wielding state power) against this petty housekeeping, or rather when its wholesale transformation

into a large-scale socialist economy begins.

....Public catering establishments, nurseries, kinder-
gartens—here we have examples of these shoots, here we
have the simple, everyday means, involving nothing
pompous, grandiloquent, or ceremonial, which can really
emancipate women, really lessen and abolish their inequality
with men as regards their role in social production and public life.[41]

In 1919, the Party created the Women's Department,
Zhenotdel—whose motto, coined by Kollontai, became "agitation by deed"—organized around two main goals. The first
was to help organize the communal kitchens, nurseries, and
laundries, which could begin to free women of the burdens
of housework.

In the first few years of Zhenotdel's existence, programs for
socializing dining and housing met with some success. Some
of the reason for this success related to the civil war's hard-
ships. For many, the choice was between eating in a communal
restaurant or not eating at all. Nevertheless, it is estimated that
during 1919–1920, almost 90 percent of the Petrograd population was fed communally, and in 1920, 40 percent of Moscow
housing was communal. Furthermore, at the Ninth Party Congress in 1920, the Women's Bureau reported that it had organized thirty-eight daycare nurseries in a province where
"women had feared nurseries like the plague."[42]

Zhenotdel's second goal was its most challenging, and in
many ways, most impressive: to help women gain the
self-confidence and experience to venture out of their tradi-

tional roles and to take part in the political life of the new socialist state. As the Russian population was still roughly 80
percent peasant, spread throughout vast rural areas, this
was no simple task. The work involved teams of organizers,
traveling on "agit" boats and trains throughout the Russian
countryside. They produced a newspaper of their own, *Kom-
munistika*. It was often quite difficult for women to step out
of their traditional roles. Particularly in the rural areas of
Central Asia, which were deeply religious, women sometimes met with violent opposition from men.[43]

Developing an idea of Zhenotdel's first leader, Inessa Armand,[44] Zhenotdel agitators organized "delegates' assemblies," in which women were elected from factories and
villages to work in apprenticeships running factories or hospitals, to serve in the *soviets* or unions, or even to function as
administrators or judges. In Zhenotdel's second year, 853
conferences of working and peasant women were held
throughout Russia. By the mid-1920s, over 500,000 women
were operating as conference delegates.[45] In the revolution's
early years, Zhenotdel took up a variety of campaigns, from
support for the Red Army in the civil war to the promotion of
education and literacy for women, with the aim of involving
ever larger numbers of women.

While much was accomplished, the years of civil war
took their toll on post-revolutionary Russia. Disease, famine,
and poverty resulted in an epidemic of homeless children,

widespread unsafe abortions resulting in illness or death, and desperate, unemployed women turning to prostitution. Zhenotdel sought to attack the root causes of prostitution—rather than penalizing its victims.

Kollontai wrote,

> Prostitution arose with the first states as the inevitable shadow of the official institution of marriage, which was designed to preserve the rights of private property and to guarantee property inheritance through a line of lawful heirs. The institution of marriage made it possible to prevent the wealth that had been accumulated from being scattered amongst a vast number of "heirs".... This is the horror and hopelessness that results from the exploitation of labor by capital. When a woman's wages are insufficient to keep her alive, the sale of favors seems a possible subsidiary occupation. The hypocritical morality of bourgeois society encourages prostitution by the structure of its exploitative economy, while at the same time mercilessly covering with contempt any girl or woman who is forced to take this path...
>
> [E]ven though the main sources of prostitution—private property and the policy of strengthening the family—have been eliminated, other factors are still in force. Homelessness, neglect, bad housing conditions, loneliness, and low wages for women are still with us. Our productive apparatus is still in a state of collapse, and the dislocation of the national economy continues. These and other economic and social conditions lead women to prostitute their bodies....[46]

The revolution's defeat

In spite of the civil war and the poverty, death, and destruction that followed the Russian Revolution, its remarkable accomplishments in the first short years of its existence gave workers around the world a glimpse of a society run by workers in their own class interests.

But the revolution's success was short-lived. Socialism is impossible in conditions of scarcity like those that plagued Russia during and long after the civil war. As Trotsky observed years later:

> It proved impossible to take the old family by storm—not because the will was lacking, and not because the family was so firmly rooted in men's hearts. On the contrary, after a short period of distrust of the government and its creches, kindergartens and like institutions, the working women, and after them the more advanced peasants, appreciated the immeasurable advantages of the collective care of children as well as the socialization of the whole family economy. Unfortunately society proved too poor and little cultured. The real resources of the state did not correspond to the plans and intentions of the Communist Party. You cannot "abolish" the family; you have to replace it. The actual liberation of women is unrealizable on a basis of "generalized want." Experience soon proved this austere truth which Marx had formulated eighty years before.[47]

The revolution's only hope for survival—the spread of revolution to some of the more industrial European countries like Germany—failed to materialize by 1923. Russia, its economy in shambles, was left isolated. Half of the working class itself either had been killed in defending the revolution or had fled to the countryside in search of food. Industrial production in 1921 had fallen to 18 percent of its 1914 level.

With the introduction of the New Economic Policy

(NEP) in 1921, a partial restoration of private enterprise aimed at economic survival, women, who had held the least skilled jobs, were the first victims. Seventy percent of the initial job cutbacks involved women, resulting in massive unemployment among women workers.[48] The Russian economy's isolation and the devastation of the Russian working class had other effects as well. The "workers' state" became increasingly staffed by bureaucrats, not workers.

From the mid-1920s on, backward ideas about women—once kept in check by the party's leadership—emerged within the new leadership of the Bolshevik Party, and came to dominate policy toward Zhenotdel. Increasingly, party leaders accused Zhenotdel of deviations toward bourgeois feminism. Its resources were cut back severely.

With the consolidation of the Stalinist bureaucracy's power in the late 1920s, the rights women had won were rapidly whittled away. In 1928, Stalin proclaimed the slogan "100 percent collectivization" for International Women's Day and called for campaigns to rationalize production, to build up collective agriculture, and to recruit women workers and peasants to the party.[49]

Zhenotdel itself was abolished in 1930. During the 1930s, abortion was outlawed, divorce became much more difficult, and Stalin proclaimed the "New Soviet Family," which meant the old "bourgeois family" with a new name. The consolidation of Stalinist rule marked the beginning of a period of massive industrialization in Russia and the brutal onset of a bureaucratic regime, bent on competing with the West. Under the sway of the new ruling class—the state bureaucracy—not just women, but the entire working class, once again returned to an existence of ruthless exploitation and oppression by the system.

Stalinism became the banner under which the bureaucracy consolidated its counterrevolution in the 1930s. In the process, the new bureaucratic ruling class turned the socialism of Marx, Engels, Lenin, and Kollontai—of revolutionary, democratic workers' power—into its opposite: state control and repression. Stalinism became a tragic example of "socialism from above" that scrapped not only workers' power, but also women's liberation. This process was personified by the transformation of Kollontai herself—from a key architect of the Bolsehvik Party's strategy for women's liberation to a Soviet diplomat under Stalin's dictatorship, fully adapting to Stalinism until her death in 1952.

It is important to understand the effects of the revolution's defeat, because many feminists have staked their case against socialism on the grounds of the existence of women's oppression in countries like the USSR, Cuba, and China. Evidence of women's oppression in these self-declared "socialist" countries, these feminists argue, proves that socialism cannot win women's liberation. But as the history of revolutionary Russia shows, Stalinism in Russia and other authoritarian regimes has nothing in common with the real Marxist tradition.

A socialist revolution in Russia brought the greatest gains for women yet seen. Only the defeat of the revolution in Russia reversed all those gains. Those feminists who offer Stalinist Russia as "proof" that socialist revolution will not involve women's liberation are missing the main point: Stalinist Russia was a class society, not a socialist country. Women's oppression within the nuclear family was as integral to the USSR—and to China and Cuba today—as it is to any capitalist society.

The lessons of 1917

The Russian Revolution was lost, but its lessons were not. On the contrary, the 1917 revolution showed the potential, if not the reality, of a society run by workers, men, and women. Alexandra Kollontai, in a passage from *Communism and the Family*, described:

> In place of the old relationship between men and women, a new one is developing: a union of affection and comradeship, a union of two equal members of communist society, both of them free, both of them independent and both of them workers. No more domestic bondage for women. No more inequality within the family. No need for women to fear being left without support and with children to bring up…. Marriage will lose all the elements of material calculation which cripple family life. Marriage will be a union of two persons who love and trust each other…
>
> Once the conditions of labor have been transformed and

the material security of the working women has increased, and once marriage such as the church used to perform it, this so-called indissoluble marriage, which was at bottom merely a fraud—has given place to the free and honest union of men and women who are lovers and comrades, prostitution will disappear. This evil, which is a stain on humanity and the scourge of hungry working women, has its roots in commodity production and the institution of private property. Once these economic forms are superseded, the trade in women will automatically disappear. The women of the working class, therefore, need not worry over the fact that the family is doomed to disappear. They should, on the contrary, welcome the dawn of a new society, which will liberate women from domestic servitude, lighten the burden of motherhood and finally put an end to the terrible curse of prostitution.[50]

In the process of building a working-class movement for socialism, the Bolsheviks had learned how to incorporate the special needs and demands of women workers into the general struggle for socialism. By putting Marxism into practice, they further developed the Marxist theory of women's liberation. They created the Women's Bureau and working women's newspapers because they understood that the oppression women face under capitalism required special methods to draw the millions of Russian working women into the process of their own emancipation.

The Bolsheviks created no *separate* organizations for women's liberation: the Zhenotdel was an arm of the party. The revolution's success challenges the notion held by many feminists that an "autonomous" women's movement is necessary to combat a system of "male power." During the Russian

Revolution, the only organizations of women that were independent of the working-class movement were those of bourgeois feminists. These were not only separate from the working-class movement, but were actually hostile to the struggle for socialism. During the insurrection in October 1917, they played a *counterrevolutionary* role, aimed at organizing an armed opposition to the revolution itself.

No organization, whatever its sexual composition, is truly "independent." Every political organization adheres to a set of ideas, political loyalties, and class interests. Separate women's organizations are not, therefore, inherently more "progressive," as the example of Russian bourgeois feminists shows. A particular set of ideas reflecting the interests of a particular social class will always dominate in a political organization. In the case of Russia, the feminist organizations held reactionary ideas, dominated by patriotism and loyalty to Russia's rulers. This is why they opposed the working class coming to power.

Furthermore, in Russia between 1905 and 1917, the special demands of women workers were raised in the context of general working-class struggle—in strike demands for maternity leave and factory nurseries, in demonstrations on International Women's Day, in riots for bread. No separate organizations of working-class women spontaneously arose during this period. Yet, the Russian Revolution represents the greatest stride toward creating the material basis for women's liberation to date.

The Bolshevik leadership, including Kollontai, was adamant that socialists' main task was to recruit women workers into the party and to integrate women workers' special demands into the general working-class struggle. To accomplish this, the party had to take up the argument with male workers that it was in their *class interest* to support demands like equal pay and maternity leave for women workers.

The Bolshevik leadership did not consider its responsibilities to involve the creation of a separate movement of women. To do so would have weakened both the struggle for socialism and the struggle for women's liberation. Separating the fight against oppression from the fight against exploitation weakens the fight against both. As Zhenotdel's first leader Inessa Armand put it, "*If women's liberation is unthinkable without communism, then communism is unthinkable without women's liberation.*"[51]

Notes

Introduction:
Is This Post-feminism—or Anti-feminism?

1   U.S. Department of Labor, Bureau of Labor Statistics cited in "Women at Work: A Visual Essay," *Monthly Labor Review* (October 1993): 48.

2   Jennifer Roesch, "Turning Back the Clock? Women, Work, and Family Today," *International Socialist Review* 38 (November–December 2004):14–15.

3   Ibid.

4   William H. Frey, Bill Abresch, and Jonathan Yeasting, *America by the Numbers: A Field Guide to the U.S. Population* (Boston: The New Press, 2001), 18.

5   Stephen J. Rose and Heidi I. Hartmann, "Still A Man's Labor Market: The Long-Term Earnings Gap," Institute for Women's Policy Research, June 2004.

6   Roesch, "Turning Back the Clock," 14–15.

7   Miranda Kennedy, "Access Denied," *In These Times* (January 8, 2001).

8   Peter Wallsten, "Evangelicals Want Bush to Reward Their Loyalty," *Los Angeles Times,* November 13, 2004.

9 Susan Faludi, *Backlash: The Undeclared War Against American Women* (New York: Crown Publishers, 1991).

10 Faludi, *Backlash*, 99–100. See also Leslie Bennets, "Myths that Men (and the Media) Live By," *Columbia Journalism Review* (January–February 1992).

11 Quoted in Edward Wyatt, "New Salvo Is Fired in Mommy Wars," *New York Times*, November 2, 2004.

12 Lisa Belkin, "The Opt-Out Revolution," *New York Times Magazine,* October 26, 2003.

13 Emma Young, "How the Cosmetics Industry Taught Us to Embrace the Knife," *The Sydney Morning Herald*, October 13, 2004.

14 Naomi Wolf, *The Beauty Myth: How Images of Beauty Are Used Against Women* (New York: William Morrow & Company, 1991), 184.

15 Megan Turner, "Why Models Got So Skinny," *Cosmopolitan* (August 2001).

16 T. Olds, "Barbie Figure 'Life-Threatening,'" The Body Culture Conference, VicHealth and Body Image and Health, Inc. 1999.

17 Jean Kilbourne, *Slim Hopes* (Media Education Foundation, 1995), video.

18 Karen S. Schneider, "Mission Impossible," *People*, June 1996.

19 Turner, "Why Models Got So Skinny."

20 *60 Minutes*, "Porn in the U.S.A.," CBS News, September 5, 2004.

21 Lori Heise, "Ending Violence Against Women," *Population Reports* (December 1999).

22 Katie Roiphe, *The Morning After: Sex, Fear and Feminism on Campus* (Boston: Little, Brown, 1993).

23 Mary Matalin, "Stop Whining," *Newsweek* (October 25, 1993).

24 Kathleen Parker, "Due Process Restored on Sex Charges," *Tribune*

Media Services, May 12, 2002.

25 Robin Warshaw, *I Never Called It Rape: The Ms. Report on Recognizing, Fighting, and Surviving Date and Acquaintance Rape* (New York: Harper & Row, 1988), 11.

26 American Academy of Pediatrics, Committee on Adolescence, "Sexual Assault and the Adolescent," *Pediatrics* 94, vol. 5: 761–65.

27 "National Crime Victimization Survey," U.S. Department of Justice, Bureau of Justice Statistics, 1997.

Chapter 1: The Origin of Women's Oppression

1 Karl Marx and Frederick Engels, *The Communist Manifesto* (New York: International Publishers, 1948), 27.

2 Frederick Engels, *The Origin of the Family, Private Property and the State* (New York: International Publishers, 1972).

3 Ibid., 10.

4 As Hal Draper agues in "Marx and Engels on Women's Liberation," in *International Socialism* 44 (July/August 1970): "There is a myth, widely accepted among the half-informed, that Morgan's anthropological work is now simply 'outmoded,' like Ptolemaic astronomy, and is rejected by 'modern anthropologists'...in this respect Darwin and Newton are outmoded as well."

5 Chris Harman, "Engels and the Origins of Human Society," in *International Socialism* 65 (Winter 1994): 84.

6 Take, for example, Peggy Reeves Sanday's argument in *Female Power and Male Dominance: On the Origins of Sexual Inequality* (Cambridge: Cambridge University Press, 1981), 210: "The evidence suggests that men and women respond differently to stress. Men almost always respond to stress with aggres-sion."

7 Quoted in Eleanor Burke Leacock, *Myths of Male Dominance: Collected Articles on Women Cross-Culturally* (New York: Monthly Review Press, 1981), 17.

8 Quoted in Leacock, *Myths of Male Dominance*, 215–31. Leacock goes on to comment, writing of hunter-gatherer and some horticultural societies, "The terminology of woman exchange distorts the structure of egalitarian societies, where it is a gross contradiction of reality to talk of women as in any sense 'things' that are exchanged. Women are exchangers in such societies, autonomous beings who, in accord with the sexual division of labor, exchange their work and their produce with men and with other women," 241. It is worth noting that the theory of woman exchange espoused by Levi-Strauss has been not only accepted, but developed further, by a layer of feminist writers. See Gerda Lerner, *The Creation of Patriarchy* (New York: Oxford University Press, 1986), 46–53.

9 Leacock, introduction to *Origin of the Family*, 31.

10 Marvin Harris, *Cannibals and Kings: The Origins of Cultures* (New York: Random House, 1977), 71–72; Leacock, *Myths of Male Dominance*, 198. See also Stephanie Coontz and Peta Henderson, eds., *Women's Work, Men's Property: The Origins of Gender and Class* (London: Verso, 1986), 17–18.

11 Sherry Ortner, "Is Female to Male as Nature Is to Culture?" in Michelle Zimbalist Rosaldo and Louise Lamphere, eds., *Woman, Culture and Society* (Stanford: Stanford University Press, 1974), 69–70.

12 Coontz and Henderson, *Women's Work*, 12–13.

13 The problem with socialist-feminist theory, however, is that it is an attempt to combine two vastly different analyses of society into a single theory. For a fuller discussion of the theoretical differences between socialism and feminism, see Lindsay German, *Sex, Class and Socialism* (London and Chicago: Bookmarks, 1989).

14 Lerner, *Creation of Patriarchy*, 46.

15 Engels, *Origin of the Family*, 71.

16 Ibid., 251.

17 Harman, "Engels and the Origins," 88. His article provides a thorough defense of Engels' account of human evolution.

18 Engels, *Origin of the Family*, 252.

19 Ibid., 38.

20 Quoted in Leacock, *Myths of Male Dominance*, 35.

21 Nevertheless, Morgan concluded, reflecting Victorian prejudice, that because Iroquois women were not given deferential treatment, they were regarded as "inferior." See Judith Brown, "Iroquois Women: An Ethnohistoric Note," in *Toward an Anthropology of Women,* Rayna Reiter, ed., (New York: Monthly Review Press, 1975), 237.

22 Ibid., 240, 249.

23 See Reiter, *Toward an Anthroplogy of Women*; Coontz and Henderson, *Women's Work*; F. Dahlberg, ed., *Woman the Gatherer* (New Haven: Yale University Press, 1981).

24 Pat Draper, "!Kung Women: Contrasts in Sexual Egalitarianism in Foraging and Sedentary Contexts," in Reiter, *Toward an Anthropology of Women,* 91.

25 Harman, "Engels and the Origins," 96–98.

26 Engels, *Origin of the Family*, 92.

27 Harman, "Engels and the Origins," 120–21.

28 See, for example, Karen Sacks, "Engels Revisited: Women, the Organization of Production, and Private Property," in Reiter, *Toward an Anthropology of Women,* 211–12.

29 Even today, it is not uncommon for unmarried women or even married women with children to accompany men on hunting expeditions in hunter-gatherer societies.

30 See Engels, *Origin of the Family*.

31 Ibid., 118.

32 Ibid., 16–17.

33 Harman, "Engels and the Origins," 125.

34 Sacks, "Engels Revisited," 216–17.

35 Karl Marx and Frederick Engels, *The German Ideology* (Moscow, Progess Publishers, 1964), 40.

36 Engels, *Origin of the Family*, 134.

37 Ibid., 121.

38 Ibid., 121–22.

39 Ibid., 119–20.

40 Ibid., 120.

41 Harman, "Engels and the Origins," 130–32.

42 Ibid., 125, 120–22.

43 Leacock, introduction to *Origin of the Family*, 41.

44 Coontz and Henderson, *Women's Work*, 119.

45 Ibid., 124–25.

46 Engels, *Origin of the Family*, 143, 98.

47 Ibid., 126, 138, 128.

48 Ibid., 131.

49 Ibid., 129, 130, 139.

50 See German, *Sex, Class and Socialism*, for a thorough examination of women's oppression under capitalism.

51 Engels, *Origin of the Family*, 137.

52 Ibid., 135.

53 Martha Gimenez, "Marxist and Non-Marxist Elements in Engels' Views," in *Engels Revisited: New Feminist Essays,* eds. Janet Sayers, Mary Evans, Nanneke Redclift (London: Tavistock, 1987), 48.

54 Juliet Schor estimates, for example, that employed mothers spend sixty-five hours per week on average performing either job or home duties. See Juliet Schor, *The Overworked American* (New York: Basic Books, 1991), 20–21.

55 Ibid., 29.

56 Sayers, Evans, and Redclift, *Engels Revisited: New Feminist Essays*, 52.

57 Engels, *Origin of the Family*, 136–38.

58 Ibid., 139.

59 Sayers, Evans, and Redclift, *Engels Revisited: New Feminist Essays*, 37.

60 Leacock, introduction to Engels, *Origin of the Family*, 15.

61 Catherine MacKinnon, *Toward a Feminist Theory of the State* (Cambridge: Harvard University Press, 1989), 19, 36, 62.

62 Lerner, *Creation of Patriarchy*, 24.

63 Engels, *Origin of the Family*, 145.

Chapter 2: Abortion Rights: The Socialist Case

1 Eleanor J. Bader, "Beyond Choice: On the Anniversary of *Roe v. Wade,* Overcoming Abortion's Stigma," *In These Times* (November 17, 2003).

2 David Stout, "President Signs Bill That Prohibits Type of Abortion," *New York Times,* November 5, 2003.

3 Physicians for Reproductive Choice and Health (PRCH) and the Alan Guttmacher Institute, "An Overview of Abortion in the United States," January 2003. Available online at http://www.agi-usa.org/pubs/ab_slides.html.

4 Rickie Solinger, ed., *Abortion Wars: A Half Century of Struggle, 1950–2000* (Berkeley: University of California Press, 1998), xi.

5 PRCH, "Overview of Abortion."

6 Marian Faux, *Roe v. Wade* (New York: Macmillan Publishing Company, 1988), 188; Andrew H. Merton, *Enemies of Choice* (Boston: Beacon Press, 1981), 36.

7 PRCH, "Overview of Abortion."

8 *Guardian* (U.S.), April 12, 1989, 7.

9 PRCH, "Overview of Abortion."

10 Quoted in Betsy Hartmann, *Reproductive Rights and Wrongs* (New York: Harper & Row, 1987), 97.

11 Solinger, *Abortion Wars*, 132; Committee for Abortion Rights and Against Sterilization Abuse (CARASA) and Susan E. Davis, ed., *Women Under Attack* (Boston: South End Press, 1988), 28.

12 Hartmann, *Reproductive Rights and Wrongs*, 111–15, 232.

13 For more current information, see the revised edition of Betsy Hartmann, *Reproductive Rights and Wrongs: The Global Politics of Population Control* (Boston: South End Press, 1994).

14 Garry Wills, "Evangels of Abortion," *New York Review of Books*, July 15, 1989. Biblical passages typically cited by anti-abortion crusaders as "proof" that Christian teachings prohibit abortion are widely disputed.

15 Merton, *Enemies of Choice*, 188.

16 Kristin Luker, *Abortion and the Politics of Motherhood* (Berkeley: University of California Press, 1984), 58–59.

17 CARASA and Davis, *Women Under Attack*, 54.

18 Ibid., 51; Merton, *Enemies of Choice*, 141–42. During the 1980s, Republicans sought repeatedly, but unsuccessfully, to win the passage of a Constitutional ban on abortion, known as the Human Life Amendment.

19 Thomas B. Edsall, "Lott Decried for Part of Salute to Thurmond," *Washington Post*, December 7, 2002.

20 Quoted in Solinger, *Abortion Wars*, 233.

21 Quoted in William Saletan, *Bearing Right: How Conservatives Won the Abortion War* (Berkeley: University of California Press, 2003), 26.

22 Solinger, *Abortion Wars*, 122.

23 Saletan, *Bearing Right*, 72–73.

24 Quoted in Saletan, *Bearing Right*, 72–73.

25 "A Step Backward for Abortion Rights," *International Socialist Review* 1 (Summer 1997).

26 Quoted in ibid.

27 Saletan, *Bearing Right*, 232.

28 *CNN Late Edition*, January 21, 2001. Transcript available online at http://www.cnn.com/TRANSCRIPTS/0101/21/le.00.html.

29 Solinger, *Abortion Wars*, xiv.

30 David Brody, *Workers in Industrial America* (Oxford: Oxford University Press, 1980), 14.

31 Ibid., 15.

32 Leslie Woodcock Tentler, *Wage Earning Women* (Oxford: Oxford University Press, 1979), 137; Johanna Brenner and Maria Ramas, "Rethinking Women's Oppression," *New Left Review* 144 (March–April 1984): 53–54.

33 U.S. Department of Labor, Bureau of Labor Statistics, "Monthly Labor Review," October 2003, 48; Eva E. Jacobs, ed., *Handbook of U.S. Labor Statistics*, seventh edition (Bernan Press, 2004), 86.

34 Bureau of Labor Statistics, 48.

35 Stout, "President Signs Bill."

36 Quoted in Patrick Healy, "Clinton Seeking Shared Ground Over Abortions," *New York Times*, January 25, 2005.

37 Quoted in Judith Hole and Ellen Levine, *Rebirth of Feminism* (New York: Quadrangle/The New York Times Book Company, 1970), 293–94.

38 Cited in Sara Evans, *Personal Politics* (New York: Random House, 1979), 221.

Chapter 3: What Ever Happened to Feminism?

1 "Wisconsin Abortion Clinics Shut Down, Citing New Law," *New York Times*, May 15, 1998.

2 "Alleged Action 'Boorish But Not Harassing,'" *Washington Post*, April 2, 1998, contains the bulk of the transcript of the judge's

ruling.

3 *Time*, June 29, 1998.

4 Gloria Steinem, "Feminists and the Clinton Question," *New York Times*, March 22, 1998.

5 Anita Hill, "A Matter of Definition," *New York Times*, March 19, 1998.

6 Susan Faludi, "Sex and the Times," *Nation* (April 20, 199): 8.

7 Ibid.

8 Naomi Wolf, *Fire with Fire: The New Female Power and How It Will Change the 21st Century* (London: Chatto & Windus, 1993), xvi.

9 Ibid., 263.

10 Ibid., 318.

11 Ibid., 57.

12 Ibid., 318.

13 Ibid., 58.

14 Ibid., 42.

15 Ibid., 57.

16 Gloria Steinem, *Revolution from Within: A Book of Self-Esteem* (Boston: Little, Brown & Co., 1992), 332.

17 Wolf, *Fire with Fire*, 51.

18 Ibid., 221.

19 Ibid., 222.

20 Ibid., 256–57.

21 *Time*, August 18, 1986.

22 Wolf, *Fire with Fire*, 141.

23 Ibid., 142.

24 Naomi Wolf, "Pro-Choice and Pro-Life," *New York Times,* April 3, 1997.

25 Quoted in "A Step Backward for Abortion Rights," *International Socialist Review* 1, Summer 1997.

26 Quoted in Healy, "Clinton Seeking Shared Ground."

27 Jane Roh, "Stakes High for Dean," *Fox News*, February 12, 2005.

28 Kate Michelman, Letter to the Editor, *New York Times*, January 27, 2005.

29 Betty Friedan, *The Feminine Mystique* (New York: Dell Publishing Company, 1963), 204.

30 Ibid., 22.

31 Ibid., 362.

Chapter 4: Women and Islam

1 Paul Silverstein, "Headscarves and the French Tricolor," *Middle East Report* (MERIP) (January 31, 2004).

2 Haroon Siddiqui, "Why Hijab Disturbs Dictators, Democrats," *Toronto Star,* February 15, 2004; "German State Bans Hijab for Teachers," Aljazeera.net, April 3, 2004, available online at http://english.aljazeera.net; and "Justice Department Challenges Oklahoma Hijab Ban," IslamOnline.net, March 31, 2004, available online at http://www.islamonline.org/English/News/2004-03/31/article05.shtml. It is worth noting that the Bush administration opposes a hijab ban. "Religious discrimination has no place in American schools," stated Assistant Attorney General for Civil Rights Alexander Acosta recently. But Bush's opposition to the hijab ban is more likely explained by his allegiance to the Christian Right, which seeks greater influence of the dominant Christian religion in schools and other public agencies.

3 Silverstein, "Headscarves and the French Tricolor."

4 Jon Henley, "Something Aggressive About Veils, Says Chirac," *Guardian* (UK), December 6, 2003.

5   Silverstein, "Headscarves and the French Tricolor."

6   Andree Seu, "By Banning Religious Symbols, Secularism Shows its Blindness," *WORLD Magazine* 9, issue 15 (February 7, 2004); Silverstein, "Headscarves and the French Tricolor."

7   Siddiqui, "Why Hijab Disturbs."

8   Ibid.; Sylvia Zappi, "'Intolerance Towards Islam' under Scrutiny by France's CNCDH," *Le Monde*, November 24, 2003.

9   Henley, "Something Aggressive About;" Seu, "By Banning Religious Symbols."

10 Paul Webster, "Le Pen Tipped to Make Big Comeback in Local Polls," *Observer* (UK), January 11, 2004.

11 Pierre Tévanian, "Say No to Racial Discrimination," *Le Monde diplomatique*, February 2004.

12 Andrew Borowiec, "A Religious Symbol of Secular Conflict," *Washington Times*, January 11, 2004.

13 Norman Madarasz, "France Starts Facing Up to Anti-Muslim Discrimination," *CounterPunch*, December 5, 2003, available online at http://www.counterpunch.org.

14 Zappi, "Intolerance Towards Islam."

15 Quoted in Janelle Brown, "Terror's First Victims," Salon.com, available online at http://archive.salon.com/mwt/feature/2001/09/24/taliban_women/print.html.

16 Mariam Rawi, "Betrayal," *New Internationalist* 364, January–February 2004, available online at http://www.newint.org.

17 Ibid.

18 Ibid.; Meena Nanji, "Afghanistan's Women After 'Liberation,'" *Znet*, December 29, 2003, available online at http://www.zmag.org.

19 Ibid.

20 PRCH, "An Overview of Abortion."

21 Quoted in Brown, "Terror's First Victims."

22 Leila Ahmed, *Women and Gender in Islam* (New Haven and

London: Yale University Press, 1992), 152–53.

23 Ibid., 153.

24 Ibid., 137, 147.

25 Ibid., 153.

26 Ibid., 154–55.

27 Ibid., 144–45, 155, 159.

28 Siddiqui, "Why Hijab Disturbs;" Behzad Yaghmaian, "Scarf and Make-up: the Modern Face of Islam. Religion and Secularism in Turkey and Iran," *CounterPunch*, February 23, 2003.

29 Ahmed, *Women and Gender*, 192.

30 Ibid., 204.

31 Phil Marshall, *Revolution and Counter Revolution in Iran* (London and Chicago: Bookmarks, 1988), 49.

32 For more information on the revolution in Iran, see Saman Sepehri, "The Iranian Revolution," *International Socialist Review* 9, Fall 1999.

33 See Ahmed Shawki, "The Bush Doctrine: Turning Point for U.S. Imperialism," *International Socialist Review* 26 (November–December 2002); Lance Selfa, "The Other War Party," *International Socialist Review* 33 (January–February 2004); and Paul D'Amato, "Imperialism and the State: Why McDonald's Needs MacDonnell Douglas," *International Socialist Review* 17 (April–May 2001).

34 George Szamuely, "Israel's Hamas," *New York Press* 15, issue 17 (April 24–30, 2002).

35 Ken Silverstein, "Blasts from the Past," *Salon*, September 22, 2001.

36 Matt Frei, "Hell on Earth: Afghanistan," *London Evening Standard,* February 20, 2001.

37 Silverstein, "Blasts from the Past;" Natasha Walter, "When the Veil Means Freedom," *Guardian* (UK) January 20, 2004.

38 Walter, "When Veil Means Freedom."

39 See Wolf, *Beauty Myth,* and Alison Pollet and Page Hurwitz, "Strip Till You Drop" *Nation* (January 12–19, 2004).

40 Yaghmaian, "Scarf and Make-up."

41 Ibid.; Nadia Hijab, *Womanpower: The Arab Debate on Women at Work* (Cambridge: Cambridge University Press, 1988), 53.

42 Williston Walker et al., eds., *A History of the Christian Church,* 4th ed. (New York: Charles Scribner & Sons, 1985), 284.

43 Bill Berkowitz, "The New Christian Crusades," WorkingForChange, April 4, 2003, available online at http://www.workingforchange.com/article.cfm?ItemID=14780; Maureen Dowd, "Head Spook Sputters," *New York Times,* April 15, 2004.

44 Ahmed, *Women and Gender,* 5, 35–36.

45 Quoted in Gwynne Dyer, "Islam Isn't Alone in Patriarchal Doctrines," *Toronto Star,* July 3, 1990.

46 Sharon Smith, "Engels and the Origin of Women's Oppression," *International Socialist Review* 2, Fall 1997, reprinted in this volume, chapter 1.

47 Quoted in Rosa Luxemburg, "Socialism and the Churches" (1905), *Rosa Luxemburg Speaks* (New York: Pathfinder Press, 2001), 194.

48 Ibid., 200.

49 Engels, *Origin of the Family,* 120–22.

50 Ibid., 13, 46.

51 Ahmed, *Women and Gender,* 14.

52 Ibid., 62.

53 "The Power to Make a Difference," in *OPDV Bulletin,* the biannual newsletter of the New York State Office for the Prevention of Domestic Violence, Spring 2000.

54 Karl Marx, "Introduction to a Contribution to the Critique of

Hegel's Philosophy of Right," (*Deutsch-Französische Jahrbucher*, February 1844), in *The Marx-Engels Reader*, Robert C. Tucker, ed. (New York: W W Norton & Company, 1978), 54.

55 V.I. Lenin, "The Attitude of the Worker's Party to Religion" (1909), *Collected Works, vol. 15* (Moscow: Progress Publishers, 1960), 402–13.

56 V.I. Lenin, "Socialism and Religion" (1905), *Collected Works,* vol. 10, 83–87.

57 Lenin, "Attitude of the Worker's Party to Religion."

58 Ibid.

59 Ibid.; Lenin, "Socialism and Religion."

60 Lenin, "Attitude of the Worker's Party to Religion."

61 See Leon Trotsky, *History of the Russian Revolution* (London: Pluto Press, 1977), 899.

62 Tom Lewis, "Marxism and Nationalism: Part One," *International Socialist Review* 13 (August–September 2000).

63 Tom Lewis, "Marxism and Nationalism: Part Two," *International Socialist Review* 14 (October–November 2000).

64 Lenin, *On the Emancipation of Women* (New York: International Publishers, 1977), 63–64.

65 Richard Stites, *The Women's Liberation Movement in Russia: Feminism, Nihilism and Bolshevism 1860–1930* (Princeton, NJ: Princeton University Press, 1978), 287; Trotsky, *History of the Russian Revolution*, chapter 39.

66 Stites, *Women's Liberation Movement*; quoted in Noel Halifax, *Out, Proud and Fighting* (London: Socialist Workers Party, 1988), 17.

67 Clara Zetkin, "Reminiscences of Lenin," in Lenin, *On the Emancipation of Women* (Moscow: Progress Publishers, 1977), 115.

68 Lenin, "The Question of Nationalities or Autonomization," *Collected Works,* vol. 36, available at http://www.marxists.org/archive/lenin/works/1922/dec/testamnt/autonomy.htm.

69 "Theses on the National and Colonial Question," Minutes of the Second Congress of the Communist International, July 28, 1922, available online at http://www.marxists.org/history/international/comintern/2nd-congress/ch05.htm.

70 Richard Pipes, *The Formation of the Soviet Union: Communism and Nationalism 1917–1923* (Cambridge, Massachusetts, 1997), 73, 77, 84.

71 C.E. Hayden, "The Zhenotdel and the Bolshevik Party," in *Russian History* vol. 3, part 2, 160, 162.

72 Richard Stites, "Women's Liberation Movements in Russia, 1900–1930," *Canadian American Slavic Studies* 7, 4 (Winter 1987): 472.

73 Adrienne Lynn Edgar, "Emancipation of the Unveiled: Turkmen Women Under Soviet Rule, 1924–29," *The Russian Review* 62, (January 2003): 132.

74 Stites, "Women's Liberation Movements in Russia," 339.

75 Ibid., 340.

76 Trotsky, *History of the Russian Revolution*.

77 "Theses on the National and Colonial Question," Minutes of the Second Congress of the Communist International, July 28, 1922. Available online at http://www.marxists.org/history/international/comintern/2nd-congress/ch05.htm.

78 Trotsky, *History of the Russian Revolution*.

79 Lenin, *Collected Works,* vol. 5, 423.

80 September 7, 1920, Seventh Session, Baku Congress of the Peoples of the East, available online at http://www.marxists.org/history/international/comintern/baku/ch07.htm.

81 Ahmed, *Women and Gender*, 163, 47.

82 Ibid., 166.

Chapter 5: Women and Socialism

1   Marx and Engels, *Communist Manifesto*, 27.

2   Engels, *Origin of the Family*. See also, V.I. Lenin, *On the Emancipation of Women* (Moscow: Progressive Publishers, 1972).

3   Lydia Sargent, ed., *Women and Revolution: The Unhappy Marriage of Marxism and Feminism* (London: Pluto Press, 1981), 7, 19.

4   Quoted in *Time* (August 18, 1986): 63.

5   Leon Trotsky, *Women and the Family* (New York: Pathfinder Press, 1970), 8, 21.

6   Engels, *Origin of the Family*.

7   Sherry Wolf, "The Roots of Gay Oppression," *International Socialist Review* 37: September–October 2004.

8   Ahmed Shawki, "Black Liberation and Socialism," *International Socialism Journal* 47 (Summer 1990).

9   Karl Marx, *Capital, Vol. 1*; Philip Foner, *The Life and Writings of Frederick Douglass,* Vol. IV.

10 See Shawki, "Black Liberation and Socialism," for a complete history of the period.

11 Nelson Lichtenstein, *State of the Union: A Century of American Labor* (Princeton, N.J.:Princeton University Press, 2002), 14–15.

12 Ibid., 213.

13 Randy Albelda, "Under the Margins: Feminist Economists Look at Gender and Poverty," *Dollars & Sense* 243 (September–October 2002).

14 Engels, *Origin of the Family*, 137.

15 Wolf, "Roots of Gay Oppression."

16 Susan Brownmiller, *Against Our Will: Men, Women and Rape* (New York: Fawcett Columbine, 1975), 14–15.

17 Ibid., 11–12.

18 Frederick Engels, *Origin of the Family*, 125.

19 Ibid., 145.

20 Michael Zweig, *The Working Class Majority: America's Best Kept Secret* (Cornell, NY: Cornell University Press, 2000).

21 Marx and Engels, *Communist Manifesto*, 18.

22 Lenin, *Collected Works,* vol. 5 (Moscow: Progress Publishers, 1961), 412.

23 Ibid., 423.

24 There is no shortage of academic literature claiming that the 1917 Russian Revolution was a "coup," and the Bolshevik Party leaders ruled as ruthless despots from the earliest days of the revolutionary government. Richard Pipes, Harvard University professor and conservative activist, has authored a series of books fueling this viewpoint, the most recent being *Communism: A Brief History* (New York: Random House, 2001*)*. Less well known, however, are numerous eyewitness accounts, which describe a flowering of democracy and the transfer of political power to workers' councils in the immediate aftermath of the insurrection. Left journalist John Reed's *Ten Days That Shook the World* (New York: International Publishers, 1919) offers such an eyewitness report of the revolutionary process in 1917. It is important to distinguish between the democratic character and aims of the revolutionary government and the rise of the Stalinist bureaucracy that ushered in a ruthless dictatorship in the late 1920s that crushed it.

25 Stites, *Women's Liberation Movement*, 287.

26 Rose Glickman, "The Russian Factory Woman, 1890–1914" in Dorothy Atkinson et al., eds., *Women in Russia* (Palo Alto, Calif: University of California Press, 1978), 81.

27 Kollontai joined the Bolsheviks in 1915 over shared opposition to the First World War. She survived the rise of the Stalinist bureaucracy, and escaped execution (most other Bolshevik veter-

ans of the 1917 revolution were executed by Stalin). Under Stalin's rule, she was appointed a Soviet diplomat, and, until her death in 1952, she accommodated to the Stalinist regime, failing to speak out against Stalinist repression.

28 Stites, *Women's Liberation Movement*, 326–28. Also see C.E. Hayden, "The Zhenotdel and the Bolshevik Party," 166.

29 Alix Holt, *Selected Writings of Alexandra Kollontai* (Westport: Lawrence Hill & Co., 1977), 44–45.

30 Alexandra Kollontai, "The Social Basis of the Woman Question," in *Selected Writings*, 59.

31 Stites, *Women's Liberation Movement*, 253–54.

32 Ibid., 257.

33 Ibid., 282.

34 Ibid., 287.

35 Ibid., 289–90.

36 Ibid., 301–04.

37 Kollontai, "A Serious Gap," in *Selected Writings*, 126.

38 Tony Cliff, *Lenin: Revolution Besieged* (London: Bookmarks, 1987), 2.

39 Quotes in J. Lauritson and D. Norsad, *The Early Homosexual Rights Movement 1864–1935* (New York, 1974); cited in Noel Halifax, *Out, Proud and Fighting* (London, 1988), 17.

40 Lenin, *On the Emancipation of Women*, 69.

41 Ibid., 63–64.

42 Hayden, "Zhenotdel and the Bolshevik Party," 160, 162.

43 See "Women and Islam," this volume, for a description of the challenges facing the Bolsheviks in Central Asia.

44 Armand died of typhus in 1920.

45 Stites, "Women's Liberation Movements," 472.

46 Holt, *Selected Writings of Alexandra Kollontai*, 262–65.

47 Leon Trotsky, *The Revolution Betrayed* (New York: Pathfinder Press, 1972), 145.

48 Beatrice Farnsworth, *Alexandra Kollontai* (Stanford: Stanford University Press, 1975), 291. See also Hayden, "The Zhenotdel," 170.

49 Stites, "Zhenotdel: Bolshevism and Russian Women," 192; and Hayden, "Zhenotdel and the Bolskevik Party," 170.

50 Holt, *Selected Writings of Alexandra Kollontai*, 258–59.

51 Quoted in B.E. Clements, *Bolshevik Feminist: The Life of Alexandra Kollontai* (Bloomington: University of Indiana Press, 1979), 155.

Index

W

Y

Z

Also from Haymarket Books

WHAT'S MY NAME, FOOL? SPORTS AND RESISTANCE IN THE UNITED STATES
Dave Zirin   1 931859 20 5   July 2005
Edgeofsports.com sportswriter Dave Zirin provides a no-holds-barred commentary on the personalities and politics of American sports.
"Zirin is America's best sportswriter."—Lee Ballinger, *Rock and Rap Confidential*

THE DISPOSSESSED: CHRONICLES OF THE DESTERRADOS OF COLOMBIA
Alfredo Molano   1 931859 17 5   April 2005
Here in their own words are the stories of the Desterrados, or "dispossessed" — the thousands of Colombians displaced by years of war and state-backed terrorism, funded in part through U.S. aid to the Colombian government. With a preface by Aviva Chomsky.

THE WORLD SOCIAL FORUM: STRATEGIES OF RESISTANCE
José Corrêa Leite   1 931859 15 9   April 2005
The inside story of how the worldwide movement against corporate globalization has become such a force.

A PEOPLE'S HISTORY OF IRAQ: THE IRAQI COMMUNIST PARTY, WORKERS' MOVEMENTS, AND THE LEFT 1924–2004
Ilario Salucci   1 931859 14 0   April 2005
Iraqis have a long tradition of fighting against foreign and domestic tyranny. Here is their story.

YOUR MONEY OR YOUR LIFE (3rd edition)
Eric Toussaint   1 931859 18 3   June 2005
Globalization brings growth? Think again. Debt—engineered by the IMF and World Bank—sucks countries dry.

THE STRUGGLE FOR PALESTINE
Edited by Lance Selfa   1931859000   2002
In this important new collection of essays, leading international solidarity activists offer insight into the ongoing struggle for Palestinian freedom and for justice in the Middle East.

About Haymarket Books

Haymarket Books is a non-profit, progressive book distributor and publisher, a project of the Center for Economic Research and Social Change.

We believe that activists need to take ideas, history, and politics into the many struggles for social justice today. Learning the lessons of past victories, as well as defeats, can arm a new generation of fighters for a better world.

We take inspiration and courage from our namesakes, the Haymarket Martyrs, who gave their lives fighting for a better world. Their struggle for the eight-hour day in 1886, which gave us May Day, the international workers' holiday, reminds workers around the world that ordinary people can organize and struggle for their own liberation. These struggles continue today in every corner of the globe—struggles against oppression, exploitation, hunger and poverty.

It was August Spies, one of the martyrs who was targeted for being an immigrant and an anarchist, who predicted the battles being fought to this day. "If you think that by hanging us you can stamp out the labor movement," Spies told the judge, "then hang us. Here you will tread upon a spark, but here, and there, and behind you, and in front of you, and everywhere, the flames will blaze up. It is a subterranean fire. You cannot put it out. The ground is on fire upon which you stand."

Visit our online bookstore at www.haymarketbooks.org.

We could not succeed in our publishing efforts without the generous financial support of our readers. Many people contribute to our project through the Haymarket Sustainers program, where donors receive free books in return for their monetary support. If you would like to be a part of this program, please contact us at info@haymarketbooks.org.